# TWO PLAYS:

*A Murder of Crows*

and

*The Hyacinth Macaw*

# Mac Wellman

ↅↄ

# TWO PLAYS

## *A Murder of Crows*
and
## *The Hyacinth Macaw*

LOS ANGELES
SUN & MOON PRESS
A PRIMARY STAGES BOOK
1994

Sun & Moon Press
A Program of The Contemporary Arts Educational Project, Inc.
a nonprofit corporation
6026 Wilshire Boulevard, Los Angeles, California 90036

This edition first published in paperback in 1994 by Sun & Moon Press
10  9  8  7  6  5  4  3  2  1
FIRST EDITION
©Mac Wellman, 1994
All rights reserved

Portions of *A Murder of Crows* first appeared in *The Kenyon Review.*
The author is grateful to the editor of this publication.

This book was made possible, in part, through an operational grant from the Andrew W. Mellon Foundation and through contributions to The Contemporary Arts Educational Project, Inc., a nonprofit corporation.

Cover: *Crows,* unknown (Edo period, c. 1650)
Seattle Arts Museum, Eugene Fuller Memorial Collection

LIBRARY OF CONGRESS CATALOGING IN PUBLICATION DATA
Wellman, Mac [John] [1945]
*Two Plays: A Murder of Crows* and *The Hyacinth Macaw*
p. cm. — (Sun & Moon Classics: 62 / A Primary Stages Play)
ISBN: 1-55713-197-X
I. Title. II. Series.
811'.54—dc20

Printed in the United States of America on acid-free paper.

# A MURDER *of* CROWS

*A Murder of Crows* received its New York premiere at Primary Stages [Casey Childs, Artistic Director] on April 22, 1992, with the following cast:

| | |
|---|---|
| NELLA: | Anne O'Sullivan |
| SUSANNAH: | Jan Leslie Harding |
| HOWARD: | William Mesnik |
| GEORGIA: | Lauren Hamilton |
| RAYMOND: | Stephen Mellor |
| ANDY: | Reed Birney |
| CROW #1: | Tina Dudek |
| CROW #2: | Ray Xifo |
| CROW #3: | David Van Tieghem |

Directed by Jim Simpson; Scenic Design: Kyle Chepulis; Costumes: Bruce Goodrich; Lighting Design: Brian Aldous; Composer and Sound Designer: David Van Tieghem; Choreography: Tina Dudek; Stage Manager: Melanie White

The author would like to thank the following for their generous support: The New York Foundation for the Arts, The John Simon Guggenheim Foundation, and the National Endowment for the Arts. The author would also like to thank the Bellagio Study & Conference Center of the Rockefeller Foundation, and the staff at the Villa Serbelloni, where this play was writ.

NOTE: The occasional appearance of an asterisk (⋆) in the middle of a speech indicates that the next speech begins to overlap at that point. A double asterisk indicates that a later speech (not the one immediately following) begins to overlap at that point. The overlapping speeches are all clearly marked in the text.

# A MURDER OF CROWS

## SCENE ONE

*A front porch of an American-type house. Only: no house. A
woman, NELLA, stands on the porch looking out. Her
daughter, SUSANNAH, stands a few yards down stage with an
enraptured look on her face, also looking out.*

NELLA:
My husband was of ordinary size and
so was the house. This part of the
country presents a problem. It don't
fit on the map right. That's because
we're downwind of the big reactor.
Not to mention the county dump, where
that hellacious grease pit is. The
rivers in this part of the state all
look like bubble baths, and the air's
all mustardy. Even the local ocean's
a little oily and waxy. Like a big
bowl of custard, wiggly custard.
When the kids were young the sea was
normal. Of the logic of the sea my
younger one, Susannah, said: It's lucky
the shallow end is near the beach.
A lot of things bore the mark of luck
upon them. Andy and Susannah were
good kids till they grew up. They
grew up just dandy till they were
done with that, then they got strange.
Andy went off to the short war in
Iraq, and came back strange. Something

7

in the air there. Susannah took the
short cut to strangeness: she stayed
at home. Something in the air here.

> *Lights up on a pair of boots protruding from a washtub.*

That's not Andy. That's dad,
and he's dead.

> *Lights up on* ANDY, *all gilded over, on a pedestal: a statue.*

That's Andy. He became beautiful
in the war.

> *Pause.*

Just look at that. Beautiful. He don't,
however, talk no more. Says the wind
and the hot and the cold of the desert
took his speaking voice away.

> *Pause.*

Beautiful. Mostly we leave him in
the garden for photosynthesis. And he makes
a fine sundial. He looks very religious
standing in the garden, even in the rain.
Now the garden isn't ours. We lost our
house. We lost the house because after
Dad died we couldn't make the payments.
Payments require cash to back them up.
Generally they do. It's an ominous thing
about payments. So we lived in various
places, with various relations who lived
variously in various places. All of them
downwind of something. It's peculiar how
no matter where you are you're always

downwind of something peculiar.

> *Pause.*

These relations were called Howard
and Georgia. They were mostly not home,
having gone for the day to the track.
They were a lucky people, and they always
came back with money.

> HOWARD *and* GEORGIA *enter with shopping bags full of*
> *money. They go up the porch steps, and out, happy.*

They didn't mind us being there, just
as long as we didn't get underfoot
and would rotate Andy from time to
 time, rotate him so he would not be
oxidized more on the one side than
the other. Now none of us we were
never a religious family except for
what you get from watching the TV,
and listening to whoever said what.
Don't get me wrong: I really think
faith is a fine thing. I really do.
If you can afford it. I really do
wish I had more of it, in my heart,
because the time comes when you wish
you did, especially if★ you don't.

SUSANNAH:
    Mother, you're talking like a
    dumb hick. Why do you do that?

NELLA:
    This is Susie, the middle one.
    Susie has a lack of respect for

9

her elders.

SUSANNAH:

You know you don't believe in nothing.
You know none of us believe in nothing.
Why do you try to cover up? It's shameful
enough just being who we are, so
why make it worse with this hollow
pretense. We live in a bubble of
sham, pure sham.

NELLA

Susie has never quite evolved from
a troubled state of adolescent development
to something higher.

SUSANNAH

I don't care what you think. I don't
care what anybody thinks, because nothing
matters anymore, but the weather.

NELLA

Susie talks like this since she came back
from Iraq—I mean since Andy came back
from Iraq and turned into a public
monument.

*An eerie pause.*

SUSANNAH

The weather is changing, the weather
is changing for sure, I can smell it.
The weather has got a whole wheelbarrow
full of surprises up its sleeve for us.
Yes ma'am.

NELLA

What *do* you mean Susie? The weather changes
every single day. Would you just explain
what you are trying to say when you make
this kind of remark?

    *Pause.*

SUSANNAH

No. The time is not ripe. The moment
will come. Everything that is vertical
will become horizontal. Seven feet, with
unusual shoes on them, will emerge from
seven open doors, doors previous locked
tight shut. X will lead Y into the night,
which will blaze up bright as day. A big
pink passle of wind will stream out of a
billowy, purple cloud and ask each and
every one of us a thing or two he'd like
to know.

    *She goes out.*

NELLA

What in the name of Sam Hill do you do
with a child who talks like that?


SCENE TWO

    *The same.* HOWARD *appears, alone, on the porch and
addresses the audience in a casual, conversational way.*

HOWARD

Nella's all right. Only she's never been
the same since the avalanche by the . . .

grease pit. Landfill, or whatever it was.
Godawful sludge heap. That ghastly, wolfish
slime. She don't like to talk about it,
and lord knows I wouldn't either.
If the shoe fits, wear it, I always
says. But Raymond never would've
come to nothing anyhow, you ask me.
Cause how you ever gonna amount to
much if you don't get focused
and put your wheel to the wall and
get a move on. I know, I know. I've
been there, the downside ain't my idea
of Christmas and Easter, particularly
when you got bubbling hot asphalt, a
whole damn lake of it, at the bottom
of the stairs. The way we did, back home
in . . . skip it. They don't talk about
*that* on the TV, nosiree Bob, they don't,
and do you know WHY they don't talk
about it? I'll tell you why because
if they did the ordinary joe in the
street would say, whoa, we do not like
the idea of this bubbly vat of hot slime
at the bottom of our basement steps, and
we are going to get organized. And there's
that word again, ORGANIZED. You remember?
It's a good word, you'd better believe it,
a word for times like these, you'd better
believe me. But Raymond now, Raymond
was all heart, all heart, but he was
not cut out for the business. He wanted
to be something else. Whatever it was
he wanted to be he never said, but it

was something else. You could tell he felt
that way because when you'd talk about . . .
well, stuff . . . important-type stuff,
you know . . . work and . . . commitment and
stick-to-it-itiveness . . . what it's all
for . . . he'd kinda glaze over and his eyes'd
get all glassy and strange.

> SUSANNAH *enters behind him, unseen.*

Like that girl of his. Strange, and wild.
Wild in a way that's out of the ordinary,
not just the usual rambunctiousness,
and letting off of steam.

SUSANNAH

Uncle Howard, the weather's going to change.

HOWARD

Sure, honey, the weather's going to change.

> *He looks at her a long time. She is lost in her reverie.*

They've been here six weeks, and I
won't say it's not been hard. It's been
hard. There aren't a lot of jobs around
here, not jobs a sane man or woman
would want to do. Who wants to cart
buckets of grease from the grease pit
to the county dump all day? Nella's
a fine middle-class lady, and it's
a disappointment for her to be in the
position she is in, of having to clean
out airplane restrooms at strange times
in the middle of the night. She and
Susie too. We fixed up the chicken coop

13

real nice for them. But still it's an
adjustment. But the way I look at it,
anything beats hauling grease from the
grease pit. Foreigners do that, people
with fezes and berets and bad teeth.
Come to think it, they must do something
like that back home where they come from.
Only where do you suppose they *do* come from?

SUSANNAH

Uncle Howard, I can really smell it now.
I really can.

HOWARD

What can you smell, Susie?

SUSANNAH

The weather, of course. You know that.
The weather's turning itself inside out.

HOWARD

Okay, Susie, if you can smell the
weather, tell me what it smells like?

> *Pause.*

Come on, tell me what it smells like.

SUSANNAH

It smells like the empty rooms of god.

GEORGIA

Are you two out here?

SUSANNAH

What does it look like?

GEORGIA

Watch your mouth, young lady.

SUSANNAH *gets up and goes out calmly.*

HOWARD

Georgia, calm down. She's only a child.

GEORGIA

Your whole damn family: subnormal.
She's not right in the head, she's
strange. Peculiar. Obflisticated.
They've been here six months, Joe.

HOWARD

Howard's the name, if you don't mind.
Joe was the name of your first husband.

GEORGIA

I know the name of my first husband
perfectly well, and I don't need you
to remind me. You're trying to distract
me from the subject of your sister and
her strange children. Well, it won't
work, I won't be distracted. Face facts,
Howard, your family is unusual, they are
unusually unusual.

HOWARD

Georgia, pipe down, what do you want me
to do, throw them out? For Christ sake,
the breadwinner was buried in an avalanche
of radioactive chicken shit, I mean
all you could see was the sole of one
boot, and you want me to throw them
out, penniless, to live on the streets?

I can't believe you are capable of that,
even with that rivet in your head, Georgia.

GEORGIA

All right, all right. I know you're right,
and when you talk like that, all you do
is further humiliate me, and that's
all right too, I'm used to it, I don't mind, I
can take it, and it won't be the first time.
Only Howard, I have a vision of how good
America could be, if only it weren't for
your family, particularly that part of it
currently residing in our house, because
America deserves better than this, I mean
this overcrowded, down-in-the-dumps,
small-time depression atmosphere, it
just doesn't hit the nail on the head,
it's not up to snuff, furthermore it's
bothersome and a crying shame. And I know
we've got to be hospitable even when we
don't give a crap, but why oh why must they
smell so bad, Jesus, Howard, it drives me
crazy, the way they stink. That's not
normal. All the people in Michigan
can't smell like that. There must be
something wrong with their insides to
make a stench like that. They're eating
our food, so it can't be that, our food
is good, normal American-type food.
Nothing too unusual, nothing too spicy.
They bathe, don't they? I mean, I've seen
evidence of them bathing, so it can't be
that. Maybe they only pretend to bathe,

is that possible? Howard, could they be
THAT INSANE that they would only pretend
to bathe, but secretly not bathe?

HOWARD

Georgia, everyone in Michigan smells
that way.

## SCENE THREE

*Nightfall.* SUSANNAH *alone outside, in front of the porch, with
a candle. Wind. Eerie wisps of light. Is she praying?*

SUSANNAH

I wish Aunt Georgia and Uncle Howard
would drop dead, sweet Jesus, or please,
PLEASE! at least be disfigured horribly
by acid, or heavy machinery. I wish
they would die very soon, and go away,
and leave us the shopping bags of money
which they have hidden I know not where.
I wish a general pox on all their houses.
Except for that part of the house we
live in, Mom and me, and the dog;—
fuck the dog!—fuck the dog, and let
him sizzle in the fires of hell also—;
but save our dear kitty Lucifer Ornamental
Pokum, dearer to me than anyone, or anything.
Because, sweet Jesus, who dwells in the
fullness of the clouds and the mist, in the
rain, in the sleet, in the snow, and even
in the rich amber filigree of the twilight,
these relations, all of them, both, are

wicked, tactless, vicious, nosy, cheap,
sleazy, cornball, sadistic even, and not
with it, not with it in a way that I find
totally . . . boring.

   *Pause.*

They do not correspond to the picture of
humanity I have formed in my head. All
they think about is local politics, the
eighth race at Aqueduct, and taxes. Taxes
and the price of oil. They think about
money too much, and are always complaining
about how they need more of it. They make
mother and me feel like freeloaders and bums
and homeless people, just because we have
no money and no place to live.

   RAYMOND *appears, menacingly, behind her, in the shadows.*

If my father
were still alive he would sweep down upon
them with his anger and fire and iron thorns
and flails, and destroy them like the Indians.
He would roar out of the TV set and leap
upon them and slit their throats, and mutilate
their bodies and roast them until they were
burnt to a crisp. Then he would stomp on
their ashes till there was nothing remaining
but a hideous black smudge on the carpet
of the living room. Living room! A place I
loathe and look down upon. A "living room"
possesses no climate in general, and no weather
to speak of. A living room is like Andy:
a useless relic of a long-gone historical

moment. I am not among my kind, and do not
even know what my kind are. I feel strange.

*She weeps quietly.*

HOWARD *(enters, listening)*
So only the weather interests me. Especially
because I know it's going to change, and
the only person who understands this is me.
Because I have a special kind of sensitivity
to changes of this kind.

HOWARD *laughs.*

Oh, you surprised me.

HOWARD
Guess I did. But I'd like to know just
how the weather's gonna change. Really!
A man could make a small fortune on a
thing like that.

*She's quiet.*

Now, now, I know you're having trouble with
Georgia, but you shouldn't let her bother
you. Just because she's a venal old biddy
with the mind of a circular saw . . .

SUSANNAH
She's a hideous, rotten cunt.

HOWARD
Yes, she's a hideous, rotten cunt. It's
true, but she's got her feelings too. Life
hasn't been too easy on her. We old folks
don't have enough to do, most of the people
we hate are dead, or sick, or locked up in

jails or nut-houses, and since all we believe
in is murder and hatred and envy of anyone
who has more fun than we do, it's rough.
You're lucky you can still get excited by
 the idea of causing someone pain, particularly
if they're colored, or an Arab, or look funny.
I know it's hard for you to imagine, but
Georgia was beautiful once, god, when she
put on her robes, at the big Klonvocations,
she was beautiful, and her bigotry was beautiful
too. Breathtaking bigotry. It gives me a
hardon just thinking about her . . . beautiful bigotry.

SUSANNAH

I'm waiting for Christ the Destroyer,
Uncle Howard, and I know He will arrive
in a storm.

HOWARD

We all have a spark of divinity within
us, Susannah. Other people can help you
find it, but you have to look within.

SUSANNAH:

It's hard, Uncle Howard.

HOWARD

I know, sweetheart, I know. You've
got to find the murder in your heart.

*A nice pause.*

Why don't you go down to the pond,
and throw rocks at frogs? That'll
cheer you up if anything will.

SUSANNAH:

  Thanks, Uncle Howard.

  *She goes out.* GEORGIA *enters.*

GEORGIA

  Where'd she go?

HOWARD

  Down there.

GEORGIA

  There's someone who'd like to have a word
  with her.

HOWARD

  Who is it?

GEORGIA

  A pelican disguised as a flamingo.
  How should I know?

HOWARD

  If I was you I'd put a lid on that crap,
  particularly as you got that damned rivet
  in your noggin.

GEORGIA

  Why don't you leave off with references
  to "that rivet" in my head. It's none
  of your beeswax.

HOWARD

  What'd you do with the money from yesterday?

GEORGIA

  What do you think I did with it? I threw it
  in the river.

HOWARD

Watch your mouth.

GEORGIA

You watch your mouth. If it weren't
for this rivet in my head we wouldn't
be eating t-bone and drinking red wine.
By the way, I got a hunch for the fifth
race at La Jolla, tomorrow. Pigs in Moonlight.
90 to 1. A sure thing.

*Pause.*

HOWARD

And who's this someone who wants to
have a word* with Susannah?

GEORGIA

Says he's the weatherman. Says he's
trying to track down a rumor he's heard,
a strange rumor.

## SCENE FOUR

*By the pond. Three big, evil-looking* CROWS *on a tree-limb in
the distance.* SUSANNAH *alone, throwing rocks at frogs.*

SUSANNAH *(she throws)*

Did you know there were no sunspots from
1645 to 1715, roughly the entire reign of
Louis Quatorze, the Sun king?

*Throws.*

Do you know there was no summer at all,
all over the world, in 1816, after the

eruption of Mount Tambora, in the East Indies?

*Throws.*

Or that just before the Battle of Manzikert
in the eleventh century, huge hailstones fell
on the Byzantine camp—each with a perfectly
preserved hepatica blossom frozen inside?
They looked like eyes. The Byzantines were totally
destroyed by their enemy, the Seljuk
Turks of Sultan Alp Arslan.

*Throws.*

I'm tired of this boring weather, I want
some other, more interesting weather than
this. People hunger for times when things
change in ways they can't predict or even
comprehend. It's the psycho-apocalyptic urge.
People need to be reminded that the simple
things they take for granted: a blue sky,
a grassy field, a glass of water, aren't
really that simple at all. Or that even the
air we breathe is a shape-shifting will-o-the-wisp.
Something in me can tell that the world we think
we know is about to undergo a terrible, cataclysmic
transformation. And that we are about to embark
on a funhouse ride that'll just get stranger and
stranger, and that when we emerge from the other
end we may not even be "people" any more; we'll
be something else, something finer, harder,
cleaner, more murderous but much more spiritual.
Matter is becoming spirit, that's what it boils
down to. And I'm going to be the one who's
going to announce it to all the world.

RAYMOND *enters.*

RAYMOND
Pardon me. I'm from the government.

*Shows her a badge.*

SUSANNAH
You're the weatherman.

RAYMOND
I'm from the U. S. Meteorological Survey.

SUSANNAH
That's what I said
you're the weatherman.

*A creepy pause.*

RAYMOND
In a manner of speaking, yes.

SUSANNAH
I've been expecting you.

RAYMOND
I'm sure you have.

*Another creepy pause.*

Nice day, isn't it?

SUSANNAH
Splendid. Indian summer. St Martin's
they call it in Europe.

RAYMOND
Yes, I know.

*Yet another creepy pause.*

There're a few questions we'd like to ask
you.

SUSANNAH

"We"? I see just you.

RAYMOND

The "we" refers to my colleagues and
myself.

SUSANNAH

There are more of you?

RAYMOND

Many more. We occupy a large building
downtown. We do many things. We record
data. We measure isotherms and isobars.
We tabulate and hypothesize. We speculate
and draw up predictions. We advise the
rich and powerful concerning the weather.
We suggest beach days for the multitude.
We insinuate ourselves into people's lives.
We congregate and murmur. Yes, we murmur
sweet nothings into the ears of those who
do not belong to our secret society. Our
society has a secret name. Our society
has a secret badge.

*Shows her.*

A secret handshake.

*Shows her.*

And a secret hat.

*Takes it out of his pocket, and puts it on. It's a crow hat.*

SUSANNAH
  Dad, it's you.

RAYMOND
  Shhhh.

SUSANNAH
  But I thought you were dead.

RAYMOND
  I have enemies in high places, so I had to
  pretend. America is not a safe place for
  people like you and me, people who have
  ideas. I have ideas about different things
  than you, but that's all right. America,
  America, is a sewer of the mind.

SUSANNAH
  But what about the accident, and how
  you were buried in slime?

RAYMOND
  That was not me, that was someone else
  who looks like me, but was not me. Actually,
  it was our old neighbor, John Q. Fedup.
  You must remember John, the man who did
  not believe in the miracle at Horsedark?

SUSANNAH
  Yeah, the guy with the scary lawn-mower.

RAYMOND
  Yes, it was a terrifying lawn-mower.

    *His aspect becomes strange.*

  I lured him into my thrall by promising
  him unusual powers.

*His aspect becomes normal.*

He fell for it, the sucker.

SUSANNAH

But why, Dad? Why?

RAYMOND

My enemies had assembled everywhere, in the
thin places of the wind even, and I knew
I must act fast.

SUSANNAH

Are you sure you're feeling okay, Dad?

*Pause.*

RAYMOND

Let's stick to the subject, and get to
the point: let's talk about the weather?

SUSANNAH

I think it's going to change.

RAYMOND

I think so too. But precisely *how* do you think
the weather will change?

SUSANNAH

I don't know. Everybody keeps asking me that.
All I know is that I feel it changing, ever so
slightly, even now.

RAYMOND

But you must have some notion of what
this change will consist of? Of whether
the air will grow thin and cold and the
glaciers will once more crunch and flatten

their way south, pushing all that lives to
seek refuge in the sunny clime of a dwindling
luxury condo diaspora. Or that the air will
grow thick and hot, and that all humanity will
expire—simultaneously crushed, fried,
and poisoned by a lethal, new climate like
that of our sister planet, Venus.

SUSANNAH

All I know is that it will be
titanic.

RAYMOND

Titanic . . .

SUSANNAH

That's right. Titanic. The whole, entire fabric
of the heavens will burst open, like a ripe fig,
and a whole new sky we never dreamt was there,
will appear. Only it *has* been there all along,
only we humans haven't been able to see it,
on account of being chronically short-sighted.

RAYMOND

And what will this new sky look like?

SUSANNAH

I told you
I don't know.

> *Pause.*

Like a sprig of blossoming mustard.

> *A tender pause.*

Dad, why don't you tell me how it
happened. I mean, how you came back

28

to life. Please. I need to know.

RAYMOND

> Okay, honey. Fair enough. If you really
> want to know. It happened kinda like this.

*The* CROWS *begin a softshoe.*

## SCENE FIVE

*The funeral: a flashback.* RAYMOND *lies in his coffin.* NELLA,
GEORGIA, *and* HOWARD *are quarrelling, all at the top of
their voices.*

GEORGIA

> He was the fucking meanest son-of-a-bitch*
> I ever met, not to mention cheap and conniving.

*She spits on the deceased.*

> All he ever cared about was his share
> of the action. Colossal son-of-a-bitch.
> And him and his shoes. Ask anyone about
> him and his shoes. Fucking biggest, dumbest
> shoes in the world. Monster shoes. Arab
> shoes. He had these *green* shoes, I mean it.
> Green like a goddam monster alligator pear.
> Absurd. He looked like a god damn foreigner
> in them shoes. What kind of standard-average
> person would go and put on shoes like that,
> and him being an American! and go and pretend
> he was like one of us, decent and normal? and
> not like one of them, Arabs or Hittites or
> monster moonmen with shoes like fucking wheel-

barrows, fucking teeter-totters. And
the hats! the hats were even worse. They were incredible,
those ghastly hats. Grotesque. Perverted.
If it's possible for a hat to be obscene, his
hats were obscene. I mean. They made you
think of things no sane person ought to think
of, ever. They were not good-looking American
hats, law-and-order type hats, or patriotic,
military hats, or socially eminent country
club or corporate hats, or even energetic
and positive-minded and youthful athletic hats, no.
These hats was weird, these hats was utterly
depraved dago moonman hats, the way they wiggled
and wobbled suggested strange fruits and unnatural
and sick proclivities. Proclivities that are best
chained to the wall of the state hospital for the
criminally insane. These hats are not my idea
of Christmas and Easter and the Fourth of July;
these hats do not go decently among school children
and farm animals with their head held high and a tear
in their eye as they sing the national anthem and
salute the flag. These hats ought to be pickled
in slime, like him, or flattened by a change in
the weather, a change of the sort that looney tunes
niece of yours has been predicting.

HOWARD

You greedy old sows, fighting like swine over
the dead, it's outrageous. We're a civilized
people. Civilized people don't act this way.
Civilized people would be acting like civilized
people; civilized people would be saying sad★
things about the dead, like how worthy and noble

they were, and how even if they never did much
in life, and were pretty much a loser—a shiftless,
untrustworthy, ne'er-do-well—, they still had a
claim on our hearts. Even if they were like
Raymond here, a total fizzle, a colossal existential
dud, a complete and laughable failure at all he ever
attempted in all his clownish, dipshit, clutzy life;
he still was a HUMAN BEING and therefore worth a
serious moment or so, on the occasion of his passing
into the murk of the next world. One hell of a crow's
world where I fear he will be an object of much
merriment among the angels and seraphim and hardbills.

*Pause. He waits till* GEORGIA's *done. He laughs hysterically*
*and starts up once more.*

But I confess I never thought much of him ever
since we were boys together at high school in
Horsedark, and he ratted on me when I looked
over Jenny Miller's shoulder and got the answer
right. He ratted and he ratted and he ratted on
me, and I was humiliated in public. I never got
over being humiliated in public, and I am a
Christian gentleman so I believe in forgiveness
and do not harbor grudges even though I'd like
to gouge the eyes out of his head like jelly,
because I may be a god-fearing American-type guy,
a small-town, happy-go-lucky Christian-type fellow
but you'd better remember I'm no wimp and if you
fuck with me you will die and I don't never forget
nothing nobody done did to me since I was ten years
old and this pathetic, crypto-commie, this alien
stooge, this human farce; this rabbit-faced, luckless
goon; this milksop; this weakling; this devious,

31

evil-minded, dirty little yellow bastard;—man I wish
I could've run him through a roaring buzz saw, or
chuck him wholehog into a MacCormick Reaper and
watch him spill out the other end like human spaghetti.

   *Pause.*

But don't get me wrong, I loved the guy.
I loved the son-of-a-gun. Why, when I
think of all the things we done together
I get the chills. Hay rides in the dark
of the moon, baseball in the poison-ivy patch,
harmless pranks on smaller, weaker, less
entrepreneurly-minded kids, and so on and
so forth; it makes me want to sit down and
cry. He was the sweetest son-of-a-gun who
ever soaked an anthill with kerosene and
then tossed the lit match.

   *He breaks down.*

NELLA

   I know, I know, I know: it's my fault.
   If only I'd been kinder, gentler more
   loving and sophisticated none of this
   would've come to pass. I know, please
   forgive me for being such a fool; I know I've
   been a total fool with my life, all of it,
   including getting poor and homeless after
   his death and having to impose like this,
   on the good will of relations, my dear
   brother and my sister-in-law, both of you,
   successful and clear-sighted and pillars
   of the community, and far above Susannah
   and me, poor folks who ought to be swept

under the rug, or otherwise disposed of,
as one would do with garbage, cat-litter
or moldy old clothes, clothes not even fit
for the Salvation army.

    *Pause.*

Fate stinks, on the whole, I would say.
Although I am proud. I am not bitter.
Bitterness is for drunkards, prostitutes,
and the unemployed who do not even try to
go out and find a job of real work to do,
as for instance, in the service industry or
something, even at the grease pit where
they hire Arabs and other Asiatic filths
because no white person will lower himself
to stoop to that horrid, putrid slime and
actually lift whole shovels-ful of the awful
stuff and drop it, ick! in the wheelbarrow
and not faint from the reek with some man in a
fez standing nearby, grinning wide, his teeth
blackened—the ones that haven't been kicked
out in fights over gypsy women, liquor and the
dice in some ramshackle Asiatic bazaar. And
him not doing a lick of work, while your heart
goes boing! boing! as if you had fallen from a
high place and hit the pavement. I'm sorry
about all of it, and I know I'm to blame.

    *Long pause as* RAYMOND *sits up in his coffin.*

RAYMOND

    Fuck you, fuck all of you. You think to yourselves
    "the old fucker's dead"; well he's not dead.
    He's not about to give you the satisfaction.

33

He's gonna get right up outa this fucking
coffin and tell you all what he thinks of you.
Fuck you, fuck all of you. Because you bunch
of dirty, shit-eating swine . . .

> *All freeze as he gets up out of his coffin, and tells them off (The*
> *freeze is more a bored-actor-standing-around-waiting-for-the-*
> *other-guy-to-finish-his-monologue-freeze than the glacial, classic*
> *variety).* SUSANNAH, *in a puddle of light, enters strangely. She*
> *touches* RAYMOND *with a wand, and he continues, also*
> *strangely.*

Y the weather goes on this way stopped
    being a question and started to sing.
Y the weather gets where it gets
    puts on its dancing shoes.
All stops are fretted to the bone, being
    sky-born and wind-driven.
Several seasons rolled in a bag.
Concentrate on the whole shebang.
Concentrate on the Y in the weather's
    eye and come up snake eyes.
Block on block.
Fend off ends.
Block on another block, dust
    in the mist closes the clock.
Types of blocks, noted.
A block without socks shivers
    in the rain, without no dance card.
Defend the cradle of memory
    from blocks of mist men.
For the blank block boots it shoe.
And fends off other eyes, other eyes than those.
For those grow monstrous in the

mythic woods.
For you who got to get, suppose the
   wrong whether and Y.

    *Pause. To* SUSANNAH.

But they weren't listening, so I waited till
later on, at the funeral home, and crept
off to live among the crows. Everyone
thought I was dead and buried, only I wasn't.
Got along fine with the crows. Crows are
fine upstanding folks if you treat 'em
with a little respect. It's a thing I have
much wondered on during the course of my
long and ratchety, rat-bitten life. Others
will behave unto you like as how you have
done unto them, and that's a fact. Even
crows and things worse, weasels even.
Godamighty, it's true.

    *They look over the frozen ones.*

But, hell, that's all history, and I'm like
you. I get this kink in my side that tells
me the weather's changing, and that makes
an optimist of me. Even if I *am* homeless,
and have lived with crows and the common people
think I died buried in chicken shit right up
to the butt end of my boot.

    *Pause.*

SUSANNAH
   Dad,★ I love you.

RAYMOND

 Hell yes, I'd still be living with crows
 if I weren't allergic to feathers.

SCENE SIX

*Just as before. Coffin,* CROWS, *etc.* RAYMOND *and*
SUSANNAH *simply walk off stage as the others break their*
*freeze. The* OTHERS *are embarrassed by the previous scene.*

GEORGIA

 I'm sorry for what I said, Nella.

HOWARD:

 I'm really shocked by what I said.
 I don't know what the devil got
 into me.

NELLA

 It's okay, I understand. Sometimes big
 emotions get bottled up inside,
 get wedged there.* And they have to
 drive a spike through the cranium,
 or drill a small hole out, out to
 the clear, bright air of the outside
 world, so you can slip a saw-blade
 through and hack your way out.
 It's not an easy thing.

HOWARD

 No, no, I feel ashamed.

GEORGIA

 We have so much. I mean, we've been
 blessed, I mean Howard and me, and

36

this kind of behavior is really . . .
disgusting.

HOWARD

Georgia here's the luckiest person
I've ever met. Roulette. Horses,
you name it. Las Vegas. Atlantic
City. Broke the bank at Monte Carlo!
Something for nothing: the great
dream of this great, big, lucky
slap-happy, lovable land of ours,
America! Craps, blackjack. It's
amazing. Professionals all assume
she cheats, but she doesn't cheat.
She don't have to! It's all luck,
by the grace of god, so help me.

GEORGIA

I mean, Nella. I never *asked* to be
luckier than you. With your face
like that, all scrunched over to
the left, and the one foot different
from the other foot. Not to mention
the life you've led,★ my word!

HOWARD

Yeah, the life you've led, Nella,
that's really been a doozy.

NELLA

Yes, it's been difficult. But I'm grateful.
I believe in inspirational literature. A
great deal of inspirational literature has
gotten me through the tough times.

HOWARD

That's really great, Nella.★ Really great.

GEORGIA

We think your bravery is remarkable.

NELLA

You do?

GEORGIA

Yes. A model. A model of something★ . . . saint-like . . .

HOWARD

Exceptional. Heart-warming. And so forth.

> *Pause.*

NELLA

Well, it *has* been hard, but I've kept . . . going . . .

HOWARD

You sure have.

GEORGIA

I never would've. I would've blown
my brains out, or jumped out of a
fifty-story window, or hung myself
from the old oak tree, or swallowed
an overdose of medicine, or slit my
wrists, or gone stark, raving mad.

NELLA

You reach the point . . . where . . . it★ . . .
doesn't make any sense anymore.

GEORGIA

Yes?

HOWARD

Go on. Please.

NELLA

I don't think I can. I think I'll
cry if I try to talk about it all.

    *Pause.*

Because the reason life was never too
easy for me was owing especially to
some peculiarities of the family . . .

    HOWARD *shuffles about uncomfortably.*

I'm sorry, Howard, but Georgia has to
hear this: you see, our family name isn't
really . . . Phillips.★ No, Howard, I have
to. It's Babaghanouj. Our great grandfather
was a . . . rug merchant from Istanbul named
Nebuchanezzar, Nebuchanezzar Babaghanouj.

HOWARD

No, no, no, Nella. Please.

NELLA

We were gypsies really. We used to go
with Mom to the Milan train station to
rob the English and German tourists.
Mom would shriek and throw little . . .
Assurbanipal—that's the name of our
younger brother, he was dead of the croup
when he was only ten, and actually we
weren't gypsies at all, we only acted
like them because we thought they were
cool and stuff. Actually, we came from

a cheesy, Asiatic, mongrel tribe, a tribe
even worse than the gypsies. Anyway . . .

GEORGIA

I really don't know what to say. I'm speechless.

NELLA

Mom would throw Assurbanipal at the
tourist, while Howard would rush up
and grab one arm, and I would rush
up and grab the other arm, and Mom
would dash in, grab the wallet
and retrieve Assurbanipal—who had
a good set of lungs, by the way!—
and we would disappear into the crowd.

  *Pause.*

GEORGIA

I really don't know what to say. And
all the time (*To* HOWARD.) I thought
you went to Choate and Yale.

NELLA

The carpet business was just a front.

HOWARD

I *did* go to Choate and Yale. But how
the devil do you think I paid for it?

NELLA

There're other stories I could tell★ . . .
Howard could tell them too, but he's
got more of a sense of modesty than me.
I guess I ought to claim up, though,
out of respect for the dead.

*Pause.*

Faith kept me going all these years. Faith in god.

HOWARD
Don't Nella, for Pete's sake. Don't . . .

GEORGIA
I always wondered why you keep all
that oriental clothing in the attic,
those fezes, those strange pointy shoes . . .

> *She indicates with her hands. Pause.* HOWARD *and* NELLA
> *indicate similarly.*

HOWARD
The shoes of our people.

NELLA
Getting back to god. I always thought
of god as a young man, covered with
thorns and spiderwebs. Much like Andy
since his return. Minus the gold leaf,
and covered all over, like I say, with
thorns and beetles and dead leaves and
things. Cheese cloth and ashes. Hair
and hairballs. Alien hair. Feathers.
Bits of paper, confetti, soot. Stuff
like that. I can't for the life of me
imagine why.

> *Pause.*

But whatever god is, he is a covered god.

GEORGIA
There's something the matter with you, Nella.

*Pause. They get tense.*

HOWARD

Now, now, let's not get excited.

*Pause. They ease up.*

I've always imagined God as a great, big,
shiny, black radio. A radio a mile square,
made out of something really light and
durable, Bakelite maybe. Like those Bakelite
radios they used to have back in the forties.
A great big cube of God the Radio . . .

*An awkward pause.*

NELLA

I suppose this all . . . must be
part of the mourning process.

*She suddenly brightens.*

GEORGIA

I think of God in a more traditional way . . .
you know, all kinda . . . like light through
a prism . . . radioactive and glowing . . .
with big hands and big toes protruding
from big sandals, leather sandals, of
course . . .

*On his pedestal, ANDY reacts to this.*

HOWARD

I think of heaven as a place like Italy
except there are no banks or movie theatres.
And it's always a sunny day. Camellias.
Hellebore. Hepatica . . .

NELLA

I would only add that all the houses
are normal houses. None of the houses
are unusual houses, with respect to
size and shape, I mean.

GEORGIA

That stand to reason. I would prefer
white colonial clapboard houses with
green shutters, but I can see it your
way. At least, if you insist on it . . .

NELLA

I'd never do that.★ It's not in my nature.

GEORGIA

Good.

NELLA

I think of the entire universe as a spot of
mildew on the leaf of a sycamore tree, floating
on thin air—in an absolutely gigantic soup tureen.

GEORGIA

I think of the entire universe as a centipede,
infinitely long and infinitely slender, creeping
in an animated fashion over a crystal ball suspended
in a . . . gelatinous void of something like . . . tar.

HOWARD

I think of the entire universe as a bowling ball
balanced on a pyramid. And that pyramid sits on
the back of a big, green turtle. About the color
of an alligator pear.

*Pause. The two* WOMEN *look at each other.*

43

NELLA

What holds up the turtle?

HOWARD

Another turtle.

GEORGIA

And what holds up *that* turtle?

HOWARD

That's very clever, young lady, but
it's turtles all the way down.

> *The two* WOMEN *look at each other. Pause.* NELLA *notices the
> coffin's empty. Georgia screams. A creepy pause.*

GEORGIA

He's gone. Where on earth did he go?

HOWARD

We'd better notify the authorities.

> *They rush off.* NELLA *looks at the coffin for a long time. She
> looks all around herself.*

NELLA

May never get another opportunity.

> *She gets in. She lies down. Pause. She sits up.*

If the shoe fits . . .

> *She lies down.*

44

*Just as before, at the end of scene five, only now* NELLA,
HOWARD, *and* GEORGIA *walk off, leaving* SUSANNAH *and*
RAYMOND. CROWS, *coffin, and* ANDY *all as they were.*
SUSANNAH *and* RAYMOND *unfreeze and begin the scene.*

RAYMOND

Y the weather begets the heart's Y, I dunno.
Some shall and some shall not and some
all the more. Whole hills of wheat and
no man shall slide low till what he love's
above. Crows jerk and juke about and the
winds wind up a medley of talkative hacksaws.
We edge near the pit, back off, and think
by baking apple pie we've got the key to
the whole shitwagon and maybe we do. Maybe
we don't. I'd love to know what the inside
of a storm feels like to be one. I really do.

But if it were up to me I'd skin the cat
with a touch more care, seeing as how the
consequences of what passes for luck at gin
rummy, poker, and horses has a strange way
of barking up the wrong tree.

*An avuncular pause.*

Now I know all this is probably
stuff you've heard before, and from the
wrong end of a television set, but I can't
help wondering Y.

*A puzzled pause.*

I can't help wondering Y and I keep can't
helping it, so help me, pigsfeet. The whole

damn cross-eyed nest of squirrels keeps
getting down on top of itself and going
screwball. Now, let's just say for the
sake of argument: you go and take a barrel
of cheese all the way from Frankfurt, Kentucky
clear to Cincinnati, a barrel of cheese
disguised as a parrot, a barrel of cheese
disguised as a pelican disguised as a
flamingo. What it comes down to is this.
What you've got is a case of the spirit
of the age, which is not particularly
understanding when it comes to strange
feet, or love, or the simple enjoyment
of a sunny day in middle of a bad winter.
The spirit of the age's got its head
wedged. The spirit of America sells
used cars to unwary pedestrians, and
they're all up on blocks. The cars,
I mean. There's just a whole lot of
old crap that would like to show itself
to you. That would like to ask you a
thing or two. A whole lot of cracker
barrel horseshit that's trying to pass
itself off as the bees-knees. A whole
lot of beer-barrel hokum disguised
as tragic cornpone, a whole lot
of small hurt disguised as big
revenge, a whole lot of flag
waving, and all of it, Y the
weather, Y the whether or not,
and it's all rolling up hill.

    *Pause. He smiles.*

SUSANNAH

I understand. I guess.

RAYMOND

Guess I do too. But I'd like to know just
*how* the weather's gonna change. Really!
A man could make a small fortune on a
thing like that.

SUSANNAH

Thanks, Dad. Thanks for the advice.
But I'm young yet and haven't got
a lifetime of experience to draw
from, so if you don't mind, I think
I'll just go on waiting for the
weather to change. It's not much
to hold onto, but it's all I've got.

*She opens an umbrella. The* CROWS *open umbrellas.*

Aside from which, I've been thinking
about what you said earlier. And just
maybe I'm *not* allergic to feathers.

SCENE EIGHT

ANDY, *who has perked up during the previous discussion about
god, heaven, etc., gets down off his pedestal and addresses the
audience.*

ANDY:

Hi Dad, hi Mom. Mom, I know you're in
there.

*She rises out of the coffin.*

I heard you talking about heaven so I
thought you might want to hear about
the real place. And it is a real place,
just like hell, though neither one's
in any book. I can see you've been
concerned about me, but there's no reason
to. I feel fine. I just don't have
anything to say. The Gulf War was
such a terrific high that I guess I've
transcended a whole lot of lower human
attributes. Things like doubt, fear,
complexity, cats and dogs, girls. And
since I've transcended knowledge and
imagination too, I don't have a clue
how this transpired. The truth is
you don't need knowledge of human things
or imagination where I am. And I know
where heaven is, because that's where
I am now. Really, and it's great.
Heaven is like the Epcot Center
or Disney World. Heaven is being inside
the cockpit of an F14 on the approach
to a nice, fat target in Baghdad.
It's a feeling you can't describe
and since you don't need to, why
bother? "Bother" is another one
of those words you don't need in
heaven. Watching that smart bomb
home in on the triple A, or parking
ramp, or bridge, or command complex
and the big blossom of golden flame
darkening the morning all around
me! That experience of bliss is

like a medieval vision of Faith
Rewarded—a pure act of wish come
true. Somehow this experience has
booted me up, up onto a whole, new
plane of existence. I'm happy here.
I have a bliss within that shines
through me. You can see that I'm
golden now. That's because I'm
closer to god than you, and getting
closer and closer. Inching nearer
the holy flash point. See? I'm
becoming a complete thing of gold.
That's the mark of true beatitude.
I am in touch with the wonders of
metallization, velocity and pure
kinetic being. Lots of my friends
are with me. They all look like me.
We're all happy. So don't worry
about me. I'm doing great. It's
just that I don't have anything
to say to you, because I've gone
way beyond where you are, which
is fine with me. I never liked
it down there anyway. I really
look terrific, don't I? Beautiful
skin is a gift from God, I guess.

*He gets back up on his pedestal.*

*Four* CROWS *(they look more like mynas or parrots than real crows: ie., they're* fake *crows) perch on a bough, discussing small things and big things.* CROW 1 *is humming the* CROW'S *Song. A longish pause. (*CROW 4 *is* SUSANNAH; *she does her best trying to pass for a crow by imitating* CROW 1.

CROW 1 *(beginning the song)*
Boom-boom, boom-boom, boom-boom,
boom-boom, boom-boom, boom-boom,
boom-boom.

CROW 2
Sometimes I think maybe we're not
doing the right things, or we're
doing the right things, but we're
doing them the wrong way . . .

> *Pause.*

CROW 1 *(singing)*
One potato, two potato, three potato,
four potato, five potato, six potato,
seven potato, eight!

> *And repeat, etc.*

CROW 3
Who gives a flying fuck?

CROW 2
It's like, maybe, at some basic
level we've confused the ontic
with the ontological . . .

CROW 3

My bill itches. Would you scratch my bill?

CROW 2

It's like I'm beginning to doubt
our epistemology. Maybe we haven't
looked into the question of the
foundation of being with sufficient
rigor . . .

CROW 3

Would you *please* scratch my fucking bill?

> CROW 2 *does so. Pause.* CROW 1 *stops the song.* CROW 1
> *starts up again.*

CROW 2

Did it ever occur to you that we
don't have to talk about things
 the way we do? All this dumb-ass
"caw caw" crap. I mean, it's
pretty goddam basic, if you ask
me. I mean "caw caw" does not
shed much light on the basic
issues of Being, nor of where
we come from, nor of whither
we are headed. Not to mention
the problem of who we are . . .

CROW 3

I don't know what you're
talking about. Everyone
knows god created our people
out of marsh gas—and the
sacred slime—along with
an admixture of mustard seed.

You only talk like this because
of your low priority in the
primal murder, not to mention
your obscure position in the
current pecking order . . .
The basic order of things
has long been established.
Our task consists of fleshing
out some of the more puzzling
adumbrations of our prophets.
Like Hardbill and Screechy.
Face it: anything else smacks
of heresy . . .

CROW 2

What about the problem of other minds?

CROW 3

Heresy. Errant heresy.

    *Pause.*

CROW 2

It's getting chilly.

CROW 3

It's that time of year. Scarecrow time.

    *Feathered pause.*

CROW 2

What if, for instance, scarecrows
have a purpose we haven't divined?
That's what I mean. Maybe we're
not using the right language, or
maybe by using the wrong language
we've only managed to redescribe

ourselves into a crows' nest
of epistemological dead ends. Think
about it! That's all I'm asking.

CROW 3

The food-marking purpose of
scarecrows has been established
from time immemorial, since the
time of the Big Book of Black Wing.
Scarecrows are the totem offering
of the Dead Ones, to us, the human beings.
It's a fact of life—like the weather—
and there's nothing problematic about
it in the least, in my humble opinion.

> CROW 1 *(and* CROW 4 [SUSANNAH]*) stop. Pause.* CROW 2
> *sighs.* CROW 1 *starts up the song again.*

CROW 2

What's the use?

> CROW 1 *stops. Pause.* CROWS 1, 2, 3, *and* 4 *start up the*
> *song and continue for some time.* NELLA *reaches out of her*
> *coffin and closes the lid.* ANDY *puts in earplugs.*

CROW 2

WAIT A MINUTE!

> NELLA *sits up in her coffin, and even* ANDY *leans over to*
> *listen.*

CROW 2

What if we are Type A entities.
That is, what if we contextualize
and explain the existences of
others but cannot, on pain of
infinite regress, be contextualized

or explained ourselves?

> *Pause. All go back as they were.* CROWS 1, 3, *and* 4 *start up the song as* CROW 2 *rambles on during a slow blackout.*

I mean, really fellas, what if we are
the fly in god's ointment and not
the apple of his eye. I mean, REALLY.
I mean you gotta think about these things,
or you'll go crazy. I mean, even the
weather's crazy when it comes right
down to it. Crazy as a loon.
It's all matter becoming spirit . . .

> *Total black.*

END OF PLAY

# THE HYACINTH MACAW
*A Lullaby for the Twentieth Century*

*The Hyacinth Macaw* was first performed at Primary Stages Company, Inc. [Casey Childs, Artistic Director] on May 13, 1994 with the following cast:

SUSANNAH  Francie Swift
MISTER WILLIAM HARD  Yusef Bulos
DORA  Melissa Smith
RAY  Steve Mellor
MAD WU  Bob Kirsh

Directed by Marcus Stern; Scenery & Lighting by Kyle Chepulis; Costumes by Robin Orloff; Sound by John Huntington; Composer: David Van Tieghem; Production Stage Manager: Kristen Harris; Dramaturg: Marc Robinson; Associate Producer: Seth Gordon; Production Manager: Andrew Leynse; General Manager: Gina Gionfriddo; Press Representative: Tony Origlio; Public Relations Director: Anne Einhorn; Associate Artistic Director: Janet Reed

The mysteries current among them,
the [ . . . ], initiate them into impiety.
—HERACLITUS.

Or he said:
"Passing to the point of the cone
You begin by making the replica.
—EZRA POUND, from CANTO XXIX).

NOTE

The occasional appearance of an asterisk (⋆) in the middle of a speech indicates that the next speech begins to overlap at that point. A double asterisk indicates that a later speech (not the one immediately following) begins to overlap at that point. The overlapping speeches are all clearly marked in the text.

Thanks to the MacDowell Colony
where this play was fomented.

## ICONS FOR SCENES

| | |
|---|---|
| WOOP: | |
| GUMS: | |
| RABBITS: | |
| EXXON: | |
| WILLOWY: | |
| TIGERTIGER: | |

# THE HYACINTH MACAW

## ACT ONE

*Sunrise by the porch of an American-type house. A* WOMAN
(DORA) *opens the door, walks out on the porch, whistling a
tune. She smiles and looks about, surveying the morning with
evident satisfaction, then re-enters. The* DAUGHTER
(SUSANNAH) *runs down the steps of the porch to the backyard,
where a clothesline is hung. She plucks the line as if it were the
string of a cello, or some other musical instrument. We hear the
sound of a plucked string (we do; she doesn't). A* MAN (MR.
WILLIAM HARD) *appears carrying a suitcase (which he does
not set down until indicated). He is dressed in an ordinary
business suit, but has loosened his tie, and his jacket is flung
over his shoulder. He has been walking for some time. He spots
the young* WOMAN (SUSANNAH) *before she realizes he's there.
When she does she freezes. An uncanny pause.*

SUSANNAH

Good morning, Sir.

MR. WILLIAM HARD

Orphans ought to be sent back
where they come from. They ought
to be beaten with sticks.

SUSANNAH

I am not an orphan,* sir.

MR. WILLIAM HARD

I didn't say you were. I was
expounding philosophy, young lady.

SUSANNAH

My parents are presently in the house,

57

asleep. Except for my mom.★ She's up
and about.

MR. WILLIAM HARD

My philosophy of orphans, my girl,
orphans in whom the urge for a true
homeland will never be assuaged.
Pneumatically speaking . . .

*Pause.*

SUSANNAH

But I am not★ an orphan.

MR. WILLIAM HARD

Indeed, the spectacle of such an
egregious orphan like you, why
disremembers me, of how and
when and wherefore★ I made this
world . . .

SUSANNAH

Mom, there is a man here who wants
to ask you something I don't know.

*(To him.)*

Are you . . . a writer?

MR. WILLIAM HARD

No, young lady, but I am a variable
in the mystic sirocco of our disbelief.

SUSANNAH

Mother, please come.

*Her* MOTHER *appears.*

MR. WILLIAM HARD

Good day to you, ma'am.

*She starts hanging laundry.*

DORA

If you are who I think you are
you can wait. Standing idle
is all your kind can do anyhow.
The rest of us must toil. Must
work against the odds. Do you
know the tale of the Sistine Woodcutter?
The one who chewed his own heart
out in anguish? Do you?

MR. WILLIAM HARD

That tale is not the one I had in mind,
and since you know it, why would I
have it in mind to tell? You don't
know me. You never heard tell of
anyone like me. All that's just
four miles of hot air, the kind the
fallen angels swore by, till they
swooped and dropped. Dropped down
with all their false justification.
What you truly know you can go ahead
and tell, but what you don't! Hell!
you can't even name the name of it.
That's why the orphans in these parts
are orphans. The name for what a
person doesn't know is a terrible
thing. I've come a whole helluva
long way just to say "hello" because
I know the full absurdity of trying

to right a wheelbarrow while you are
sitting in it, ass planted North.
Land of evening. Land of the Adversary.
Do you understand?

DORA

Not one word. In this part
of the country it is customary
to jawbone a little on the subject
of the weather. Sure, jawbone
on the weather . . .

*Working at the clothesline.*

That and talk of vacations, photos
of friends and relations while
doing the best we can to not
bring up the subject of who
did what. Got cancer and died
of it, or broke back tumbling
down the cellar stairs. We are
polite. We are polite out of need.
Sweet, sweet reasonableness's need
to catch no ill crutch of roach.
So, save your★ Sistine Woodcutter's gab.

SUSANNAH

Mom, he said I was an orphan. Why
would he say a thing like that?

MR. WILLIAM HARD

He would say so to mark time.

DORA

He would say so to mark time, all
because he doesn't know how to

be properly appalled. Laundry's wet.
I don't see him so close to what
engenders. Wettens. Nor to what dry cleans.

SUSANNAH

He looks like . . . I don't know . . .
Something sheer awful.

MR. WILLIAM HARD

The truth is, I was looking for orphans,
but found you. Forget what reason was
behind it all. Took a bus, took a train.
I've had some hard times. Been had,
so to speak. Messed up with politics,
which I never had no talent for.
Simple speaking has always been my
mosthow there shitfor. Certainly.

DORA

So: are you saying you are hearing
what we are saying, or not? Which?

MR. WILLIAM HARD

I am hearing what you are not saying,
which is what I came here for, and
you two, both. It figures, because
I am from far away, a place you'd
never recognize. Bug River, the sign
here says. I'd never post that. It'd
be too much an abject certainty, and
I'd be like to lay about and grow . . .
tantamount. Same as a big, horror bug,
all myself a whorled mystery. Cheesy.
See, where I come from's on no map.
You could call me Vincent Hat, or

Johnny Sock, but the real name, the
one I answer to unquestionably is
"Mister William Hard." That's my moniker.

SUSANNAH

Bug River has nothing to do with bugs.
We have a gym, a school, malls, all
the normal things. American-type things.
We act as if nothing strange had ever
occurred here, which it has-fucking-not.
I want to attend Junior College next Fall
and learn the names of things, packaging.
Packaging's got a true forward momentum.
I believe in it. That's the metaphysical
reason I don't equal an orphan. That's
my philosophy of drift. Mom's too.
Right, Mom?

DORA

Right too, Squeezre.

MR. WILLIAM HARD

A kid's name.

SUSANNAH

So what. It's mine.

MR. WILLIAM HARD

It's yours all right.

SUSANNAH

Yes, it is. Mine. All mine. All I got, practically.

*An awkward pause. All shift about. Another pause.*

MR. WILLIAM HARD

That means I was right. You

*are* an orphan. A yanked-up
rootless thing. Adopted.

DORA

She's not adopted, she's adapted.
Squeezre, go get the man a road map
while I make him a sandwich. He
must've mislaid his topology.
Going to be too hot today for conversation.
Besides, you don't know anything, and
Mister "Johnny Sock" seems to know it all.
Therefore you're matched for life, and
oddly so. Therefore, too, you're safe
with him, the way I see it,★ so I'll
just go . . . .

SUSANNAH

Mother, you are extremely uncouth.

DORA

Squeezre, be quiet. You're rattling the bugs.

SUSANNAH

Yes, and I suppose you don't!

DORA

Behave. Show respect.

SUSANNAH

Respect is for the birds.

DORA

The man's a stranger.

SUSANNAH

Our family's more stranger.

DORA
So: behave. Be quiet.

SUSANNAH
Our strangeness must show. It's got to.

DORA
It must be hidden.

SUSANNAH
Explain what you mean.

DORA
Hidden things can be healed.

SUSANNAH
Hidden things are hurts.

DORA
Healing takes time. It's slow.

SUSANNAH
Hurts too are slow. They also grow. Slowly.

DORA
Behave. I'm your mother.

SUSANNAH
We are both human people.

DORA
Sometimes I wonder.

MR. WILLIAM HARD
Maybe you are crows.

DORA
Keep your two cents out of this please.

MR. WILLIAM HARD
Yes, ma'am. Sorry.

SUSANNAH
I demand to say what I will.

DORA
Demand anything.

SUSANNAH
What do you mean?

DORA
While you're here you'll behave like one of us.

SUSANNAH
So I am an orphan!

DORA
That's ridiculous!

SUSANNAH
It's true. Say so. Admit.

DORA
Why would anyone adopt a person like you?

SUSANNAH
I've had an inkling this was true.

DORA
Just because you can do basic reasoning.

SUSANNAH
I knew all along★ I was different. Separate.

DORA
Now you're an embarrassment. Stop.

SUSANNAH

Separate. Apart. Out of place.

DORA

Stop.

SUSANNAH

An entrechat of enthymemes.

DORA

Stop talking strange.

SUSANNAH

You're strange. I'm normal.

DORA

You're an enigma. Behave. Quick.

SUSANNAH

Okay. Okay. Quick. It goosewillies me.

DORA

Squeezre?

SUSANNAH

Quick. Behave. Stop being a . . . a girl.

DORA

Behave. Stop. React.

SUSANNAH

Quick. Okay. Stop. Okay. Goosewillies . . .

DORA

Are you listening to me? Squeezre?★ Are you?

SUSANNAH

I am listening to a different drummer★ and it . . .

DORA

Squeezre, for Christ's sake, be quiet.

SUSANNAH

It tells me to honor the quick and the dead.

> *She plucks the clothesline. We hear it. Pause. The music is atonal. Aleatoric. Non-Chekhovian. The* MOTHER *goes out (or, rather, in).*

MR. WILLIAM HARD

Progress. Progress has come to the land of evening.

> *He goes to put down his suitcase, but hesitates. Pause.*

Mind if I put this down, young lady?

SUSANNAH

Squeezre's the name if you don't mind.

> *Pause. He stands straight up.*

MR. WILLIAM HARD

Mind if I tell you the true tale of the Sistine Ornithologist, Squeezre?

SUSANNAH

My name's not "Squeezre." That's my nickname.
An intrafamilial verbal sight-gag. Old hat.
Boring. When I was a toddler I used to squeeze
up my face and hands. Like this.

> *She demonstrates.*

Or so I was told. Hence: Squeezre. My
name is Sue. Susannah. You're a stranger,
so act normal. You are acting too strange
for a stranger. You are acting truly

strange. Like family almost. Goosewillies
me . . .

*Pause. He puts down the suitcase.*

Besides, I know the tale of the Sistine
Woodcutter. Besides, I've got a full
dance-card. An entrechat of enthymemes.
So make it quick.

MR. WILLIAM HARD
The Bird-maker flew in with the wind
one day. The same wind that bears the
mystic seeds from China. Which died
with sun-up, as it's wont to. Promised
a new dispensation to the assembled
quacks. All odd ducks, people. Tribe
of paradox. So-called humanity. They
were at sixes and sevens. Gabbled amongst
theyselves. They took it he was a Woodcutter instead of a Bird-maker. In the
gloaming, his shadow clawed across
them like a tool. A terrifying implement.
An axe to grind . . .

SUSANNAH
Ha. Ha.

MR. WILLIAM HARD
You laugh.

SUSANNAH
La. La★ la.

MR. WILLIAM HARD
You laugh, and they did too. The suckers!
All they craved was the drug of authenticity.

Sad self-similarity. But he was a true
Bird-maker. Apocalyptic. Sistine. Even
a little *lupine*. Wolfish, that is. But
the world of gradualness is a sucker for
images. The resistless clamor of the new
world for images of itself. It's own folly.
Follow me?

SUSANNAH

Can't follow the thread of your . . . tale.
La. La.

MR. WILLIAM HARD

Because it is a deliberate tangle. So.
True tales are tangled. Especially in the
evening. Especially in the land of evening.
Mind if I smoke?

> *She rolls a cigarette. Gives it to him. Lights it for him. He*
> *smokes. Pause. Both look over their shoulders at the sun. Both*
> *turn back. She snaps out of it, as if out of a spell.*

SUSANNAH

Now, why in hell did I do that? I don't
even know the man.* I don't know how
to roll a cigarette. I don't even smoke.

> *She rolls herself a cigarette, and lights it while he continues.*

MR. WILLIAM HARD

So: Even came. Eventide. The Evening of
Sixty Days. He spoke in the darksome
wilderness. He convinced them their joys
were nothing but gloom inverted, sophistries,
invented geegaws, idolatries from a former
world. He said they knew not from whence

69

they ushered. Nor what dark wind uttered
them. Feathered them, and put them all
in cages. Up on perches, like a brace of
hyacinth macaws. Cockatoos. Cockatoos,
hornbills and toucans. Cockatoos of cockatrice.
In the old birdpark at Jurong. Forever chattering.
Chatting twaddle. Entrechats of enthymemes,
as you put it, in the language of your town.
Gradual, population 1990. Circa now.

SUSANNAH

And then?

MR. WILLIAM HARD

He took up archeology and flea circuses.

SUSANNAH

No I meant the people he changed. What
happened to them?

MR. WILLIAM HARD

That remains unrecorded. An historical
ellipsis. An error in the wilderness
of what we suppose we're here for, but
don't know. The outcome is lacking in
the element of decidability I mean.

*He puts out his cigarette.*

SUSANNAH

Now Mom's mad and I'm to blame.

MR. WILLIAM HARD

For shame.

SUSANNAH

You're mocking me. You have no right to.

MR. WILLIAM HARD
   Indeed. I have no rights period.

SUSANNAH
   Just what are you driving at.

MR. WILLIAM HARD
   What's real has no name. None.* Whatever.

SUSANNAH
   What?

MR. WILLIAM HARD
   None. What's real, that is.

SUSANNAH
   What's that supposed to mean?

MR. WILLIAM HARD
   You asked me. You go figure. Now you know.

SUSANNAH
   I know nothing. Mom's right about that.

MR. WILLIAM HARD
   Neither do I.

SUSANNAH
   What's your name again?

MR. WILLIAM HARD
   Bill. Bill Hard.

        *She holds out her hand. They shake hands.*

SUSANNAH
   Hi, Bill, I'm Sue.

MR. WILLIAM HARD
   Hi, Sue, I'm delighted to meet you.

*Pause. They smile.* MOM *enters. They unshake their hands.*

DORA

You still here? Thought you'd be off by now.
Squeezre, don't you have errands to do?

SUSANNAH

Yes, ma'am. Feed the neighbor cats.

DORA

Then go do it. Sun's coming up. Now.

SUSANNAH

Yes, mother.

DORA

Right now.

SUSANNAH

Okay. I'll go. Goodbye, sir.

MR. WILLIAM HARD

Good evening, young lady.

*Off she goes. Pause.*

DORA

So what is it you've come for precisely?

MR. WILLIAM HARD

Time to get around to it, I suppose.

DORA

I'd say so. And? So?

MR. WILLIAM HARD

Appears to be a case of of pneumatic
redundancy. Unnecessary replication . . .

*Pause.*

## DORA

When it becomes clear to you I'm sure
you will let us know. It would be a
shame not to. We have a right to know.
Things do happen slowly around here.
Knowledge sprouts as slowly as the mystic
seeds from China that Mad Wu talks about.
One thing about the devil, he moves fast.
Knows all that's on your mind before you
do. Take Susannah, our daughter, now.
She has signed a ninety-nine year lease
to feed the neighbor cats. I don't
know how long they'll be away. Years for
certain. Our neighbors are missionaries
in . . . some far place. A long-playing
record of woe, disease, drum-playing,
taboo, bamboo and vice. Maybe China.
Maybe Shenango. Years aplenty. Maybe
not a whole century, but it's the idea
of responsibility that works on you, grows
like a worm in a green apple. Susannah'll
grow up with this daily task until . . .
marriage, a job at the crocodilarium,
or junior college. Already I can sense
a change in her. I think I can, in only
six years. Her eyes have changed color,
from grey-green to topaz. What she says
makes more sense, and her vocabulary's
improved. She uses words like "redundant,"
"paradox" and "pathological" now. Before
she fed the neighbor cats she never would've
used a word like "pathological." Except
to spite me, or someone else. Eldridge,

or Sandoval, the man with the thing in his
backyard. The thing that goes *whump,
whump* when he winds it up. At night
when he puts on his raincoat, and
lights all those lanterns. He runs all
around his house shouting, and the big
heavy thing, it's made of iron, I suppose,
it goes *whump whump*, and then it goes
*clank clank, clang*. And then he sings:
"Hallelujah" and takes off his trousers,
and runs three times around the house, in
the rain, in his boxer shorts. That's
what he does. I am not sure what it all
means, only it must possess a . . . signification.

MR. WILLIAM HARD

I'm sure it must. Sounds like a
device like the one I witnessed back in
back in, was it Powerdive?

DORA

Oh yes. I think I remember that. Yes,
it was Powerdive. East Powerdive.
It was Mister Phelps who invented it.
He never showed it to anyone. Called
it an "Equilateral Spiritual Triangulator."

MR. WILLIAM HARD

I have some papers here in my pocket . . .
somewhere . . .

*He fumbles about in his pockets.*

DORA

I was madly in love with Mister Phelps,
when he was young and Harry . . . So

74

was I, young and Harry . . . Oh, not that,
Harry Phelps was his name. Also invented
the thing that you put in the wheelchair
between the wheelbug, and the wheelwhang.
"The whang provides the necessary whammy,"
he used to say, Harry. We would go for
long walks on the bank of Bug River, talking
about what the Adversary was up to, what
happens when the coffin is too big for the
hole; or at night in the zoo when the
big cats can't get to sleep; what life
would be like without a set of fixed
points to navigate by;

    *She looks down.*

. . . and prolonged abstinence, and how it
feeds the fires of belief. Harry talked
a lot about the value of prolonged abstinence
and the relation of this to the fear of the
world. True trepidation. Then we would
take off our clothes, wade off in the
river, and listen to the larks and jays
rattling about in the reeds and grasses.
Rattling about in the cat-tails and willow.

    *Pause.*

I have always thought that faith
had more to do with moments like that.
Long-playing moments like that. Long-
playing loganberry moments with nervous
fingers and no longevity. Moments of
pure revelation, regarding a birth mark,
a scar, another person's belly-button . . .

Never mind ministrations of the dying.

*She snaps out of it.*

You don't need faith to do the dying
in a foul bed, howling. You don't need
faith to crush the neck of a woodpecker
with a broken wing the cat brought in
to the wilderness of the kitchen in a
fit of patriotic fervor. You don't need
to grasp the full profundity of god's
love to know what's got *you* in its jaw,
shaking you to death, when it does.
When it's your turn, there is no escape.
There is no escape. That knowledge
is as sexual as all the hennaed works
of wicca, where devil fucks devil and the
long greensnake yawns and whips the wind-
tasting feather of his lolling, laggard,
lazily-serene lizardtongue. You don't,
in my opinion. You don't.

*He hands her a letter. She takes it. She looks up at him. He
gestures for her to open it. She does. It take her a long time to
read the letter. He shifts from foot to foot. Adjusts his necktie.
He looks at the sunset. Pause. He looks at his watch. Finally
she looks up. Pause.*

What does "tantamount" mean?

MR. WILLIAM HARD
    To amount to as much.

DORA
    What does "to amount to as much" mean?

76

MR. WILLIAM HARD

It means that the force of the malfeasance
has the same effect as.

DORA

Oh. I see. I guess.

*She looks a little bewildered.*

MR. WILLIAM HARD

You have to go on a bit. It becomes clearer
towards the end.

*Now he looks confused.*

Oh, I didn't give you the other page. Shit,
where is it?

*Looks in the envelop.*

Not there.

*Goes through all his pockets.*

Nope. Shit.

*Looks sheepish.*


DORA

What is "tantalum"?

*He recites the following while he goes flapping and flailing
through the tall weeds and grass near the house. She looks at
him, totally mystified.*

MR. WILLIAM HARD

A very hard, heavy, gray metallic element
that is exceptionally resistant to chemical
attack below 150 degrees centigrade. It is

used to make electric light-bulb filaments,
electrolytic capacitors, lightning arrestors,
nuclear reactor parts, and some surgical
instruments. Atomic number 73. Atomic weight
180.948; melting point 2996 degrees centigrade;
specific gravity 16.6; valences 2,3,4,5.

DORA

What about six?

*He stands up, in the middle of poison ivy, in a fury.*

MR. WILLIAM HARD

WHAT ABOUT SIX? WHAT THE HELL DO YOU
MEAN!?

DORA

Does Tantalum also have a valence of six?

MR. WILLIAM HARD

Did I SAY it had a valence of six?

*Irritated pause.*

DORA

Well, no, I thought it might, though.*
I mean, it doesn't seem all that implausible
to me. If 2,3,4,5, why not six? You tell
me, I don't know. Okay. Okay. Just
drop it. I don't care. I really don't care.

MR. WILLIAM HARD

If it HAD a valence of six it would say so
in the letter. Does it say so in the letter?
No, therefore tantalum does not have a valence
of six. Okay? Where did I drop that damned
second page? Shit.

*Stands up in horror. She goes back to the letter.*

What happens if I left it back at the
office? They'll crucify me. They'll raise
hell, and I'll never hear the end of it.
Shit, now my rotator cuff is acting up again.
Again, I should've had it taken care of when
I still had Elective Surgery through Blue Cross
Blue Shield. I did not believe Herb Shorter.
That'll teach me always to believe! HERB SHORTER,
I SWEAR I WILL ALWAYS BELIEVE IN WHAT
      YOU SAY,
WHATEVER IT IS, NO MATTER HOW
      IMPROBABLE IT SOUNDS,
ALWAYS LORD HEAL ME HEAL ME. HEAL ME IN
      MY
UNBELIEF.

*He falls down and we see only the soles of his shoes. Pause. She
still looks puzzled. His head pops up.*

You must be thinking of plutonium. Plutonium
has a valence of 3,4,5 *and* six. Plutonium
 is a naturally radioactive transuranic
element occurring in uranium ores, and
produced artificially by neutron bombardment
of uranium. Plutonium has 15 isotopes with
half-lives of  20 minutes to 76 million
years. It is a radiological poison, specifically
absorbed by the bone marrow. When exposed to
the open air, plutonium catches fire.

*Pause. Finds the page in his hat. Jumps up, delighted.*

DORA

> What is a "tarboosh"?

MR. WILLIAM HARD

> Found it! Finally. What'd you say?

DORA

> What's a "tarboosh"?

MR. WILLIAM HARD

> A brimless, felt cap with a silk
> tassel. Usually red. Worn by Moslem
> men, either by itself or as the basis
> of a turban. Here's the other page.

> > *He hands it to her, and while she reads this, he dusts himself
> > off.*

DORA

> What's a "taradiddle"?★ Jesus, you
> do find some *hard* words . . .

MR. WILLIAM HARD

> A "taradiddle" with one "r" is a variant
> of "tarradiddle" with two.

DORA

> That doesn't clarify matters much.

MR. WILLIAM HARD

> A "tarradiddle" is a petty falsehood. A fib.

DORA

> You are accusing my husband
> of perpetrating a fib?

MR. WILLIAM HARD

> I am not the author of this document,

only its deliverer. Deliverer of its deliverance.
Forgive me. I bear no responsibility for the
contents of this message. It derives from a
higher authority, an authority beyond rebuke.

DORA
Oh . . .

    *Pause.*

In that case, I guess I'd better call
up Ray at the office and find out
what this is all about.

    *She looks at him.*

I hope you don't mind if I leave you.
Would you like a cup of coffee? Or a
cheese sandwich? Looks like rain.
You might want to find shelter
under that stand of poplars. I'd
ask you in, but under the circumstances
I don't think I will.

MR. WILLIAM HARD
It's all right, ma'am. I understand.

DORA
You do, sir?

MR. WILLIAM HARD
Yes, I do. I think.

    *Long pause.*

DORA
Tell me, sir . . .

MR. WILLIAM HARD
  Bill Hard's the name, ma'am.

DORA
  Tell me, Mister Bill Hard. Do you
  think the deep woods of the human soul
  is full of terrible music?

MR. WILLIAM HARD
  Yes, I do, ma'am.

DORA
  So do I. Furthermore, I do also
  believe all things have happened
  before. Even the things we are not
  aware of, down in China, down there.

    *She points.*

MR. WILLIAM HARD
  So do I, ma'am.

DORA
  You do, really?

MR. WILLIAM HARD
  Yes, ma'am. Really.

DORA
  I'll be back in an hour or two.
  We've got to get to the bottom
  of this, Mister Hard. Soonest mended.

MR. WILLIAM HARD
  Soonest mended, ma'am.

    *He tips his hat. She looks hard at him.*

DORA

Who are you? Really.

MR. WILLIAM HARD

All in good time, ma'am. All in good time.

*She turns.*

DORA

I guess. Well. Okay. See you later. Don't
go anywhere.

MR. WILLIAM HARD

I'll be here, ma'am. Sunset is nice.

*He points. Sure enough the sun's going down. A slow,
picturesque black-out.*

I'll be here. In the nettles and hollyhock.
Sunset is fabulous, in the weeds and ivy.
With my heart in my throat.

DORA

See you later then.

*Slowly she makes her way indoors. Pause.*

MR. WILLIAM HARD

Good evening, ma'am.

*We hear roars from the neighbor "cats."*

END OF SCENE.


NEXT SCENE *[scene the  ⬅ (woop)]. Inside the house. The
MOM (DORA) sits at kitchen table drinking coffee. DAD (RAY)
has returned home from work. He wears a normal business suit,
but seems dazed. He slowly reads the letter she has shown him.*

83

*A starry night outside. In the woods a hunger moon is rising.*
*We can barely make out the silhouette of the* MAN *(*MR.
WILLIAM HARD*), standing motionless among the trees and*
*bushes outside.*

RAY

Okay. Okay. So when I was a kid
I went crazy, and they hauled me off
to a nut house.

    *Pause.*

I had written and staged a perverted
drama in boarding school. It was called
SENSITIVITY, OR THE LANGUAGE OF DREAD.
It contained many perverted passages
dwelling on the topic of lips and thighs.
And other torments and temptations.
Torments pertaining to the sex drive.
Torments which surround us. And convey
animalistic urges to us all, with
their laughing little wicked voices.
The persons of the play had foreign
names. They wore the fez, and performed
unspeakable acts. "Don't ever write
another play," the Headmaster suggested.
But I did, not heeding his warning. I
simply couldn't control my diabolical
urges. I was caned, canned, drummed
out. I was conveyed to the House of the
Mad in a conveyance, and talked to by
serious men concerning the Adversary,
and the diabolical nature of my urges.
I would talk to them about my fantasy

84

of performing certain unspeakable acts
while wearing a fez, or tarboosh;

*She looks up in recognition.*

They would continue to look serious,
and recommend a long period of abstinence.
I did not know what they meant by "abstinence"
since I bore the full weight of my urge
like a gigantic boulder upon my back.

*He looks down.*

Then I discovered the world of higher
mathematics, and was healed. Now
I am a perfectly normal fellow. Stable.
Always, as you have no doubt perceived,
in control. My urges have largely abated.
The urges which have not abated I have
largely trained; I have tamed them with
patience, and little sweet gifts, cookies,
chocolates and the like. My urges look up
at me now, with dark, lustrous adoring eyes.
My urges nuzzle about my trouser pockets,
and rub lovingly against my pant-leg. My
urges no longer are of the School of Night.
They no longer worship the Adversary.
Through prolonged abstinence my urges
have become model citizens of my soul,
as you and I, Dora, have become model
*citoyens*, so to speak, of the town of Gradual.

*He looks up.*

All my urges, except one. You and I
know which one, don't we, Dora?

*He whispers into her hair. She looks down.*

Don't we know the fierce temptation
to enact the urge which only the
Evil One dare pronounce? Don't we,
Dora?

*She looks up.*

DORA

But that has nothing to do with
this, dear. The letter makes no
mention of your former condition,
your urges, nor your adolescent
episodes of theatrical dementia.

RAY

It makes no mention of it, but the
implication is clear enough.

DORA

You're being paranoiac, dear.

*He looks out the window and sees the* MAN. *She looks out the window and sees the* MAN. *Pause.*

RAY

And that, I suppose, is the fellow
who delivered the letter?

DORA

Under the circumstances I didn't think
it was appropriate to invite him in.

RAY

He doesn't look dangerous.

DORA

He tells very interesting stories, and
has a boyish glint in his eye. I rather
like him. Even though he is the one
who has delivered this letter to us.

RAY

Where is Squeezre?

DORA

She is feeding the neighbor cats.

RAY

Why does she do that?

DORA

It strengthens her mettle.

*Pause.*

RAY

What is "mettle" again?

DORA

Any of a category of electropositive
elements that are usually whitish,
lustrous, and in the transition metals,
typically ductile and malleable with
high tensile strength.

*Pause. Still puzzled.*

RAY

What does Squeezre need high tensile
strength for? She's a girl.* For Pete's sake . . .

DORA

Don't be obtuse, Ray.

RAY

It shouldn't take her all day to feed a couple of cats.

DORA

There are more than a couple of
them, and some are large.
Bulky and large, one might say.

RAY

Bulky and large? Really? I wasn't
aware of that.

DORA

She'll be back before too long, I'm sure.

*A pause of uncertainty.*

I suppose.

RAY

I don't know, Dora. It gives one cause
to stop and think. You get a letter
that is mostly incomprehensible, but the
basic meaning of which seems to be—
or boils down to—basically something
like: " . . . your soul has spontaneously
combusted, foop, just like that, and
wiggled up the chimney in a wispy,
dark orchid of soot, where it shall
disperse among the lesser elements,
in particulate form . . . or . . . gas . . . ";
and, well, it gives a man reason to
stop and mull over the meaning of his
life. It makes one feel a tad uncertain.

DORA

I'm sure it's just an unusual set

of phrases for something quite familiar.
Like death. Or taxes. Or transubstantiation.

RAY

Like death?

DORA

Like not paying a parking ticket maybe.

RAY

And what's all this stuff about
"the presencing of beings" as opposed
to "Being" and "whydahs" and "moonsucking
wigglies?"

DORA

Ray, I can't tell you. I don't have
the expertise. The man in the poison sumac out there . . .

*She points. The* MAN *very slowly scratches his arm.*

. . . he has the expertise. He knows.

RAY *looks hard at the* MAN. *Pause.* RAY *turns back and sits
down.*

Ray?

*No reply. He just sits there.*

RAY

It's *déjà vu* all over again.

*He gets up and strides out. Strides back in again.*

Interesting day at the office anyhow.

DORA

How so?

89

*He sits down carefully, so no reply again. Pause.*

RAY

*Déjà vu* again. Wow! Oh, at the office?

DORA

You brought it up, not me.

*He looks puzzled.*

RAY

Oh yeah. I know what I was thinking . . .
I was somewhere else for a moment.
Strange . . .

*He looks strange.*

I've become obsessed with coincidences
lately. And today, there were no coincidences.
So—isn't this ironic—I felt safe.

*She talks as if in a trance.*

DORA

Why don't you go and ask the gentleman
what the meaning of his message is.

RAY

Funny, the same thought just occurred
to me. Funny how the obvious solution
to a problem is invariably the last one
to enter* one's mind . . .

*She is stern:*

DORA

Do it now, Raymond.

RAY

What's his name, by the way?

DORA

Mister William Hard, Doctor of Divinity,
Equidistance and Gradualness.

> *Pause. He cheers up.*

RAY

At least I'll be dealing with an educated
person.

> *She looks at him hard.*

RAY

Okay, Okay.

> *He goes out, slamming the screen door. She looks out the
> window for a long time, as the two* MEN *talk. She turns back,
> in a trance.*

DORA

. . . tarboosh . . .

> SUSANNAH *enters, wearing a fez. She sings her song [BUG
> RIVER]:*

Till the Bug River bears away
   my blues
I'll be there for you.
There in the air, with my smile
   and miles of high hopes hooray.


Till Bug River washes away
   my things,
I'll be there for you.
There in the air, with my wings

high, miles and miles above the hay hooray.

But . . .
When old Bug River fouls her nest
  I promise
I won't be there for you.
You'll have the blues; all the rest
  of us will fly away hooray hooray.

        SUSANNAH *sails once all around the kitchen and exits. Pause.*
        *Her* MOM *snaps out of whatever state she had been in.*
        *Blackout. Sudden crash of noise, and bizarre sequence of lights*

        *All (including house) up to full, and white. Then red and*
        *violent, veering through the spectrum to violet and blue, then*
        *black again. Another crash (based on the plucked clothes-line*
        *motif of the First Scene). We see* DAD *(*RAY*) in the door,*
        *looking amazed.* MOM *and* DAUGHTER *stand opposite,*
        *together. They regard him with horror. A long pause (outside,*
        *the* MAN *has vanished).*

RAY
  . . . he talked to me about various things . . .
All in a foreign language . . . Mimbreland . . .
the land of evening . . . of how the moon
was wont to come and sit before him . . . on
her footstool . . . like an amiable ghost . . .
but now is dying . . . an invisible college
of demons has instructed him . . . and all
about us, crows perched on hoodoos, a
murder of crows . . . witnesses to what was
said . . . ". . . according to necessity,"
he said, "for they pay one another recompense

and penalty for their injustices . . . " The
moon is very sick.

*Snaps out of it.*

It boils down to this, the long and short
of it, that is:

*Pause. He sits heavily.*

He is me. That's right. He is me.
I am him.* I'm a double. A duplicate.
An inauthentic copy. I'm supposed to
pack one light suitcase. Three pair of socks.
One hat.** Leave my credit cards behind,
because he'll need them.

DORA

Whatever did you do wrong, Raymond?

SUSANNAH

Father, how is that possible? How can
a heavenly body, a huge thing made out of
stone, get sick? I don't buy it. Nope.
Not me.

RAY

I am to pack a few things, and depart.
I am going far away. To someplace
he calls "the land of evening." It
turns out there has been an error in the
big plan. His friends are my enemies,
and vice-versa. My animalistic urges
apparently have nothing to do with
it. Even prolonged abstinence would
not have changed things. Much.

DORA

I'll go make you a sandwich.

SUSANNAH

Dad, what is "Mimbreland"?

RAY

The land of evening.

SUSANNAH

What is "the land of evening"?

RAY

Mimbreland. Don't ask me to explain.
I can't. This is really quite a shock
to my system. Sheesh.

SUSANNAH

Dad, can I have your credit cards?

RAY

No, Squeezre, sorry, but they belong to
him. He is me. I told you. I am him. A duplicate.

DORA

I called up Jack at the office.

> *Pause.*

He said you did things. That you were
a premature-something-or-other.

RAY

Well, yes, maybe. That might be★ true . . .

SUSANNAH

Dad, does that mean you're a fake?

RAY

I prefer the term he used. A duplicate.

SUSANNAH

Then you are a fake.* An imitation. A cheap knock-off.

RAY

Good God, Squeezre, allow me a
shred of self-respect, won't you?* Sheesh . . .

SUSANNAH

Sorry, I was just trying to establish
the facts. I have rights too you know.

DORA

Did you do the things at work, the
things Jack said you did, did you
Raymond? Did you?

RAY

Jack should talk. Jack is gaga.
Today at work Jack said, "This
is today" and I said, "What do you
mean?" and he said "Just that:
This is today" and I said, "Jack,
I don't see what you're driving at,"
and he looks me right in the eye and
says, "I had a revelation. The Angel
of the Lord came down out of the sky,
during my lunch-break, on a park bench
in Gooner Park and said: 'This is today,
Jack, and you are so lost in your
block-headed corporeal swinishness
that you cannot respond with an
open heart'. And that is what I am
saying to you, Ray: This is today.

This is today, Ray, and you are so
lost in your block-headed corporeal
swinishness that you cannot respond
with an open heart. Respond to an
utterance of purest, unblenched revelation.
This is today, Ray. Think about it."
Then he went all cross-eyed and kinda
googly, took off his clothes, right
down to the shoes and stockings,
and went all around the room, singing an
old song from yesteryear's Top 40, I
forget, doing the Rumba.* "This is today."
Can you believe it?

> SUSANNAH *holds up a huge* BUG *and stands motionless in a*
> *vatic pose, eyes skyward.*

DORA

He said you did things, that you did things
indicating something the matter with you,
in the head. He said you always had an
excuse along the lines of this was only
coincidental and that also was only
coincidental, and that appearances deceive
and that eating red meat did not imply a
moral condition involving torpitude, animalistic
boffing* of teenage sluts and so forth, and
one's status as a premature-anti-something-
or-other; but I don't buy it. I don't buy
it at all. And neither does Squeezre; do
you, Squeezre? Do you? Pay attention, dear,
this is important . . . Is that some kind of
stag beetle you've got there!? Get it away
from me, you nasty child. Get it away . . .

SUSANNAH

Does this mean I can bring my beetle
collection downstairs? Yes? No? Maybe?
Why doesn't anybody listen to me? Isn't
anyone curious to know about my life?
Doesn't anyone care about what my day
 is like, feeding those cats next door?
Those bulky, monstrous cats. With their
big, greenish, unblinking saucer eyes.
The tufts of fur on their eartips. Their
deep guttural purring, and the swishing
of their tails as they tear apart the carcasses
I fling down to them. And the huge bugs
I find in the walls, and in the wainscotting
of the neighbors' house. Big ones, like this!
Stag beetles and Rhino beetles and rare
Longhorn beetles that are not supposed to
grow in these parts. Beetles sprouted
from the mystic seeds that I found in
that shop. Seeds from China. Where Mad Wu
was born. Under a Ding-Dong tree. A
worshipper of cats and bugs and beetles.

MOM *hisses at* RAY.

DORA

Don't you say a word against Jack. You shit.
He's a beautiful loving man with a
Christian soul, and a fine set of his
own teeth. He works hard. He dreams on
things other men merely guess at. You aren't
fit to lick the shit off his shoe.

RAY

Jack's okay.

DORA

Jack understands circumstantiality,
and he respects me.

RAY

I did not mean to denigrate the man, Dora.

DORA

When Jack enters the room, things of
a wispy nature gather, outside, under
the eaves and palpitate in the moon's
spittle. And I recall my girlish circum-
rotation. The circumflex of my innocent
ardor . . .

RAY

. . .

DORA

. . .

RAY

You do?

MOM *lowers her head.*

DORA

Yes, I do.

DAD *gets up, and leaves the room. He speaks from off.*

RAY

Where's my old suitcase?

DORA

In the attic.

*We hear the attic door squeal.*

SUSANNAH

Careful. I've got beetles up there. In cans
and bottles.

DORA

Careful, Ray. She's got her beetle collection
up there.

> *A muffled yell. A muffled thump.* RAY *appears with his
> suitcase.*

RAY

My god what EYES they have. I never knew
insects could look at you that way.

SUSANNAH

I hope you didn't hurt any of them.

RAY

No, dear, I didn't.

DORA

So when do you go?

RAY

Tomorrow, I guess. After dinner.

DORA

Shall I get something special at the butcher?

RAY

Sure, leg of lamb maybe.

SUSANNAH

Can I go now?

RAY

Sure, go.

*Pause. He looks around, gets up and finds the letter. He sits down and reads it once more.*

What does "tantalum" mean?

DORA

Damned if I know. Doesn't sound very nice.

RAY

. . . sheesh . . .

*Slow blackout.*

## ACT TWO

*[Scene ⇔ (gums)] The kitchen again. Again, it is evening, the next night. Table-cloth, candle-light and a wonderful meal spread out. Sweet music from the old victrola. Toasting and merriment. The* MAN, RAY, DORA, *and* SUSANNAH. *It is* DAD*'s going-away party. Suddenly, the* MAN *becomes silent and stares at* RAY. *He (*RAY*) raps his wine-glass with a spoon. All become silent and look at* RAY. *Pause. He realizes it is time for his farewell speech. He rises from the table, glass in hand.*

RAY

Ladies and gentlefolk. Kind sirs and colleagues.

*Pause.*

Welcome to the banquet. My farewell
solemnity, and solenoid. I propose
to salute you, wife (Dora), daughter
(Susannah), good friend from the Outer
Dark (Mister William Hard) with a sally
of good cheer, a solfatarra of deeply
felt verbal solfeggio. Tonight, my heart
is full with shreds, folded pop-ups, and
the stuff of the heart, farewell stuff,
feathers, obscure bones of small creatures,
portraits in lockets of the lesser Popes,
poop, sailboats, sentimental threnodies
from the gaslight era, odd riffs of jazz,
corny keepsakes, tufts of hair, confederate
dollars sewn into the ruffles of antique
gowns, ferrotypes of audacious perukes,
satins, lizard-skins, coral buttons, ivory

needles, silver thimbles and billets-doux
from the Pretty Times Done Did.

*Pause.*

My mission has been modestly to amuse,
bemuse and defuse. I have, to the best of my
abilities, struggled to maintain a full
larder, a cheerful parlor, and a backyard
free of pests and vermin. I chose the low
way because it seemed, to me, in my dreamtime
myopia, more noble. My political thoughts
have remained primitive, but most passionately
embraced. I am a simple man beset with heart-
break. Work has been my therapy. Mathematical
unction the charm of my meat-wagon. When you
grasp the simple truth: how all things have,
well, have happened once, or more than once,
before; the fur under your collar is likely
to flatten, and not flare up, so bristly.
Such perspective ennobles the atrocious,
authenticates the truly tragic. We can
traipse into the gasworks furnace of Fate
with a gleam of what's holy in our eye, thankful.

*He looks down. He looks up.*

I am . . . simply . . . aghast. For nothing ever
cries out from its true heart to me, without
my having held my hat in my hand, looking at it,
thinking it was not mine, but someone else's.
A gift, on loan. Nothing ever flies into the
plate glass of the picture window, and plops
down, thus, stunned, to the ground, without my
feeling a pang as of a pulled weed flung into

the sky, flung with great urgency, as if the
Evil One were watching from his Tower of Tantalum,
perched there on the fiery coast of Hell, his devilish
picnic laid, with cheeses, devilwine and so forth;
there, where the heart yields to weird compunction.

    *Pause.*

I see myself a feckless youth hardened by
prolonged abstinence and chilblains, aghast,
alone, in agony. I see myself, a young shoe-
salesman on the windy plains of West Gradual,
where the Bug River hyphenates the mighty Ohio
with its moxie doodle, a cipher, a tragic hipster,
a tramp. I encounter the notorious Mu Factor
in the sad, shanty towns of Shenango and deem
myself wise with the leer of unholy knowingness.
My cynic heart fructifies the loins of my undoing
with condoms, cigars, saltpeter, and cryptic
notes inscribed on paper towels in the cafeterias
of Junior Colleges at Shenango. I treasure the
bricabrac of the sacred Mu Factor, as I torment
the Moon with my offtune whistling.
*Lira lira, lira lara, lira-lay.*

    *Pause.*
    SUSANNAH *and* MR. WILLIAM HARD *look at each other,*
    *then down.*

I complete my studies in Celestial Mechanics.
My dissertations on Clovis Man, and on the Creeping
Dartworm are published in the *Darkwind Almanac.*
The world west of Gradual stretches out before
me, like a rumpled bed full of golf balls. Clutching
the horrible inner truth of the Mu Factor, I am

able to grow fabulous greensward from what was
yellowish, pale, and covered with spikes and thorns.
I am able to perform certain amazing rites, rites
in the bleak char and firelight, all before the
foul nest of Promise, that lady of cheat. All my
doubts are as nothing to a nope star. I fear
no one. I thunder as I touch the earth with my pods.

    *Pause.*

Alas, the theory of the Mu Factor is refuted by
David Braithwaite, and his Meso-thermal Crabwise Digitator,
or M.C.D. What am I to do, a heretic with no heresy?
An inane loose screw. Useless. Arcane. Alone.
So, I look down upon my shoes, gather up what
remains of my sour circumspection, add a circumflex
to my name, learn to trot the Hilda, get up, clear out,
set off for the big cities east of here, with their
racket, wisecraft, perverted alleyways, alien custards,
bizarre hats, diddle-shoots of double-edged disregard,
and resolve to go among them, the people who dwell in
those parts, a fey joker of ill-report. A shoe-salesman
of cosmic proportion.

    *He drinks a glass of water. The others shift about in the*
    *interval. He prepares to begin once more. Rapt attention.*

From the depths of my heart I curse David
Braithwaite, and all his works. Waving my hands
to the dim roof of heaven, I will a monster
furunculosis on his abdomen, which in the
fullness of time does appear, aborting both
him and his joy. By my will, hosed down the sluice
of the Evil One's infarction.

*Pause.*

Whether wrongly or rightly, I capsize morally.
I grow contentious, arrogant, addicted to the
kind of overdrive that afflicts those hobbled
by a tender sprain, spiritually speaking. The
ball in my pivot pops out and bounces away,
under the dining room table and hops out the
screen door. Gone. Gone forever, like all
baubles the heart grows fond upon, under
variety's banana frond. We are fools, to whom
the usages of what wiggles make wilely, with
painted stripes of Oriental wickedness. Oil
lamps, tents swooshed by the sweet simoom,
fezzes and incense, wicked ankle bracelets
of the seductress. The works of temptation.

*He gulps, looks strange.*

And so, the fire of my animalistic urges
is fanned, flies up and flaps madly out the
door. In Shenango's greasy bar rooms I
enact vice. I practice my vice with surgical
precision. I practice my vice till I carry
it around with me, carry it at all times
like a hump. My depravity, my animalistic
urge to prey upon those whose goodness or
beauty or teasing, sexual tarradiddle freezes
my heart in my throat like a stovepipe hat
on the head of a nineteenth century missionary
buggering a disciple in the saturated frangipani
glade of an isle sacred to strange gods, gods
with scissors who snip the clothesline of
causal connection wherever they perceive,

in the humid air of paradisiacal archipelagoes,
a sexual suction.

*Pause.*

Such are the powers of the animalistic urges
that torment me that I struggle, like Jacob,
in the grasp of the Divine Greco-Roman. Philosophy
means nothing to me, nor commerce, nor letters.
My resolve to question and to acquire, through
prolonged abstinence, the mantle of Intellectual
Hero and Demigod flattens out; and the swerve
of my second, sad undoing is accomplished.
Feverish, I jeer goodness, frankness, well-
argued narrativity. Whenever faced with truth
and sincerity, I invoke the sarcastic raspberry
of my disbelief. I do not reckon, dear friends
and family, how all things have been done before.
Done before in the precincts of a finer, better
world, with tighter tolerances, glossier paint,
and more in the way of enhanced structural impeccability.
In short, cheesiness afflicts me in all my works, and
I am dead to nuance, timeless elegance and the rigors
of three-year limited warranty. The little clock of our
father's perfect plan has, to my jaundiced eye, petered
out in the pudding. The wreck and the lure of what's
wrecked tempts me to a perception of this world as an
instance of itself only, a green bower in a green glade,
and not a paradigm, as it truly is, of the place beyond
error, where ergo equals a Coulomb Field in which every
point is so charged with forced electromagnetic energy
as to stand directly proportional to the total, combined
product of their charges, and inversely proportional to
the square of the distance between and among them. An

infinite ergo of ergots, the consciousness altering
black bread of Mimbreland . . . Photostated in Heaven,
by the angelic horde . . . So, I snivelled . . .

*He crouches and leers.*

I snivelled, and sniggled, and sneaked away.
I smoked and niggled and slaked my lust. I
quenched the hot pods of my animalistic urges
wherever suction would permit. I perched, small,
on a remote psychic abscess of myself, ran
up and down the creaking celestial staircase,
and double-charged for half-a-plate. Nothing
foreign was not natural to me. My disciples
resembled me in their easy ways, witless saunter
and careless discharge. Cigarettes, polkas,
pinkie rings of horn and nitre, obscure deals,
black shirts and pink ties, vacations in fat lands
paid for by Bug River's most brazen delinquents,
money in stacks, bottles of acquavit, revolvers
by Smith and Wesson, lotto tickets and trick dice,
expensive shades in gold frames, stolen art works
from Eastern Europe, hen's teeth and panda's thumbs,
stuffed owls, maculate three-deckers, pneumatic
superinflatibles, bluestreak disinterments, lace,
lurchings, engineered fuddles, nude beaches, rigged
sameness, reified urchins, dead mice, scarabs, scat.

*He sits down, completely run out of steam.*

MR. WILLIAM HARD
    The optic on all that, brothers and sisters,
    is the pornographic.

DORA

As we burn, so are we quenched.

SUSANNAH

Why, when he talks like that,
about himself, does Dad employ such a
fixed vocabulary?

DORA

Hush, dear, it's your father's going-away
party, and he's had little too much to drink.

RAY

All I'm saying is I don't understand.
I wish someone could illuminate me,
that's all.

MR. WILLIAM HARD

Raymond, there is a season for quickening
and a season for puzzlement.

SUSANNAH

No one else's parents, my friends at
school, talk like this.* It goosewillies me.

RAY

What are you talking about, you ninny?

MR. WILLIAM HARD

We are all orphans, beneath the hieratic
balloon of the blank. Children of nightdoingness.
Abandoned.

*This doesn't help anyone. Pause.*

SUSANNAH

Why was Dad talking about his urges like
that? The big cats I feed next door, they

don't whine all the time about how . . . well . . .
animalistic they are. Those big cats just
glow and glisten. Their deep purrs rumble
in the twilight like a faraway lawnmower.
I hear a powerful mower in those purrs.

DORA

He's not who he thought he was, so
it's plain, he's just got to go, Squeezre.

RAY *(dazed and blank)*

He is me. I'm a duplicate. I am him.
Show's over. I'm to go to some place
called "the land of evening."★ Mimbreland.
We received notification yesterday. I am
him, whoever that is.

SUSANNAH

But why does he have to make such a big
deal about it? When I went to Indiana
nobody made such a big deal about it.

DORA

That's because he's not coming back.

SUSANNAH

Why not?

> *Pause.*

Never?

MR. WILLIAM HARD

That's right, Squeeze. A man has to take
a thing like this standing up. It's a
body blow for sure, but he's got to stand
there and take it. And not run away . . .

*He looks at* RAY *who is mouthing a wordless supplication to* DORA*, but she doesn't understand what he is trying to say. Pause.*

DORA

It's as if a very proud and important-type
American man called and asked for you.
But since you were not the person who
answered the phone, this big-type
person, someone in a position of real
responsibility; someone with values,
convictions and a complex, but highly
distinguished Curriculum Vitae, this
person got disappointed; got fed up,
and hung up. But tried again later,
only to get the same result. And kept
calling up, but since you were never
the one to answer the phone, he would
not leave the message that would save.
And because he kept calling and calling,
and leaving no message you start to get
anxious, worried and a bit perturbed.
In fact, Squeezre, you start going
through the Seven Stages of Mourning
because you start to feel like someone
you love has passed on, while you're
doing something bad in the barn, with
someone . . . foreign . . . Someone big and
stiff, with a fat lip, broken teeth,
and a really tasteless demeanor. Maybe
a fez, or tarboosh . . . You've never
had that feeling, have you, Squeezre?

SUSANNAH

. . .

> *She looks at* RAY. *He looks back.*

RAY

. . .

MR. WILLIAM HARD
I have a little present for Raymond,
on the occasion of his departure.

> *Takes out a little shiny black box. All lean over it, so we have a
> hard time seeing. All, except the* MAN, *involuntarily fall back.
> It's a very bright, vermillion snake. It is very beautiful and very
> alive.*
>
> *Pause. All are transfixed, except* SUSANNAH, *who leans
> forward to stroke it. She makes an odd noise of pleasure in her
> throat.*

SUSANNAH
Can I have one too?

MR. WILLIAM HARD
This one's for your father.

> *But he's in a trance. As if, he sees the truth, in all its naked
> power. All eye him as he slowly stands. He stutters:*

RAY
. . . Shakespeare lived in this house. This
is Shakespeare's house. He wrote all his
books here. The one about geese. The
one on gardens. And the one about the
cemetery business . . .

> *Pause.*

. . . calling up and leaving no message . . .

> *Pause.*

He cried. She cried.

> *Pause.*

He took his trousers off.

> *Pause.*

MR. WILLIAM HARD
I gave you the snake because I'm from
the Land of Evening. We worship snakes
in the Land of Evening. And that's where
I'm from, and that's where you're going.

> *He takes off his trousers. Pause. He hands the trousers to* RAY.
> RAY *looks at him, looks at the trousers, looks at his wife and
> daughter, looks out at us. Slowly, he takes off his trousers and
> hands them to the* MAN. *Pause.*

RAY
. . . and of course the one whose name
I forget. The one with that song. The
one that goes . . .

> *Suddenly he goes blank. Pause. He snaps out of it, puts on his
> new trousers (so does the* MAN), *adjusts his tie, puts on his
> jacket; and, as if unaware of the others, slips quickly and
> quietly out the kitchen door. At this point all freeze for a second
> or two.* MOM *produces a pitch-pipe from her pocket. Squeaks
> out the correct note, and all three sing, ever so softly, and with
> great, slow solemnity "The Battle Hymn of the Republic."
> Pause.*

*[Scene, the next:* 🐰 *(rabbits)]* SUSANNAH *and* DORA
*unfreeze, look about, make their way downstage and casually
hang out, smoking and talking. This scene, thus, amounts to an
odd, little interlude. While the* WOMEN *talk the* MEN *can move
around, stretch, etc, as comfort dictates. If necessary the* WOMEN
*may take their chairs downstage with them. This is a quiet,
deliberate scene. Both do a lot of thinking in between their
replies.*

SUSANNAH

Why did Dad have to go away?

DORA

Sometimes Susannah, you can row
out to the middle of Bug Lake.
And sometimes when the water is
very clear you can see all the
way to the bottom. And sometimes
when you look down what you see
there is a cause for . . . for anxiety
and fearful speculation. When
Raymond looked down to the bottom
of the lake, he saw a human face.
He recognized the face. It was his own.

SUSANNAH

I know where I am right now, but
where did Dad go? Is it far away?

DORA

The time comes when you hear the music
from another world. You know the
music is from another world because
it is so sad and strange you feel
as if you had awakened from a dream,

flung your fists out in a nightfever
and caught a living sparrow in your
hand. Only, the bird sings a piercing
wildnote threnody that drives you
unwilling straight to the center of
things. Its little heart trilling the
mysterious work of the heart. Your
father, Raymond X, Raymond X Dogsbody,★
knew this work, but could not name it.

SUSANNAH

But our family name is "Moredent."

DORA

I know, dear. I know. I was only
making an example, an example of his
instance.

SUSANNAH

. . . oh★ . . .

DORA

To go nameless in the heart's wonder
is to be a ghost. The ghosts all live
in a thin, hard place, hidden behind the moon.

SUSANNAH

If he doesn't like the food there, what will
he do? Are there places where he can go to
work if he misses his friends and colleagues?
Will his enemies go there too, and find him
out? Will he find another wife, and love
her, and make another child with her, holding
hands with her silently, of a summer's eve,
on the glider, on the front porch, with a
picture of the furnace of infinity emblazoned

for both of them, like a wilderness of competing
sunsets, at all the compass points? Will they
conceive and give birth to another child,
one like me? Will this one like me come
in the softness of the afternoon, and replace
me, systematically, in the hearts of those
who know me, who love me, who would kill to
protect me? Would she do all this in the name
of wormwood? In the name of what has not been
fathomed because it exceeds dimension, and
rushes off the spectral palette of all colors
we see, and hence of all things we know?

DORA

Wherever he is, he will awaken every day, and
every day he will catch the sparrow in his bare
hand, the sparrow of his own undoing.

SUSANNAH

So where do we stand, do we truly dwell
in the world we know, here in the town
of Gradual, on the marshy flood plain
of Bug River? Or is it all a bad joke
perpetrated on us by blue jays, a sham, a hoax?

DORA

No, it is not what we think, at least
I don't think so. But there are many things
of which I am uncertain. This is one of them.

SUSANNAH

But then, where? I need to know?

DORA

Half way through my life, I sat down and
cried because I knew, somehow, somehow

so obscurely that I could not fathom it,
that my life was half over. But at the
same time, I had the revelation that my
wretchedness would be compensated for.
That I should henceforth discover in
my heart the place of bounty. A place
where all the parallaxes of the parlous
are fused. The Holy Flame of victory
has welded my nameplate to this unwobbling
hub. So I am fixed here, and yea! my
tents are pitched forever by the waters
of sweet Jordan. Jordan River. Hallelujah!
In the land of evening. In the land beyond
the mathematical deconstruction of the soul.
Hallelujah!

SUSANNAH

Does this place have a name, beyond the inkling
of spiders? Or is it all like moss? Or like
fur? Or worse, is it like a coat of clothing
we can put on, and take off, at will? What
on earth did Dad mean by all that stuff?

DORA

I don't know. I don't know anything.

SUSANNAH

Sure, you do, Mom.

DORA

No, darling, I don't. To some, like me,
the human heart is as opaque as a stone.
Through a glass darkening your eye, there
is only the reflex perception of a glint.

I sometimes think of that glint as the first
morning of the world.

SUSANNAH

So, you *do* know something!

DORA

It is only a bauble thing. Like a singleton
earring from a cotillion ball of long ago. The
Pretty Times Done Did. An ivory earring of
error flung, hopeless, in a squat, stone box
of deepest jet. Useless. Classic. Mute.

SUSANNAH

Have all things truly happened before?
Even Dad's removal and departure?

DORA

Only the loving know no repetition. I think
it is a great mystery of the heart. The miracle
of lovingkindness was told once, only once
and that in Olden Times and sadly no one
listened. That is why crows, of all birds,
have inherited the earth. Wastrel crows,
with hearts of pitch, given to scandal-mongering.

SUSANNAH

Does anyone love me for myself truly? Did
Dad? Do you, mother?

DORA

No, my dear, no one does. You are merely
an idol of my conceit. Your father, Raymond,
loved you for yourself only, but look where
it got him. He was a silly, old man. He was
a silly old man even when he was twenty-three

years old, wore bowties, and ventilated
strawhats.

SUSANNAH
So you don't know where we are?

DORA
I love all maps, but not for what they tell
me of the world. The world is a useless thing,
without the soul's commission. Maps tell me
the mind of humankind's a porridge of whim,
wisecracks, whimsy and flim-flam. World's
only a tinny usufruct. We die in a ditch
alone, spat upon by our social betters.

SUSANNAH
But mother, I have seen the map with the
town of Gradual written all over, and Bug
River too. A sharp, red snake of a wriggle.

DORA
The devil put it there, to delude the mapmaker.

SUSANNAH
But why?

DORA
He owed him dark blood, I suppose. The blood
of senseless sacrifice. You think too much. You
can't love anything, a man, a woman, a cat, a
skink, if you think too much. Thinking poisons
the well with choke cherries and skunk cabbage.
In our time the presencing of beings has outmoded
Being itself.

SUSANNAH
What kind of people are we then? Who are

we? and why do we talk like this? Can't
I catch the sparrow in my dream, and will
my life turn out better than his? Why did
he ruin his career as a shoe-salesman
with his mad dream to climb to the stars?
What do we know truly, if we can't even
verify what's on the plate before us, at
the Holy Banquet? Are we phantoms, birds
of prey? Or are we only machines that
rattle on all through the night because
we can't turn ourselves off? Are we going
to be hosed down the sluice, with David
Braithwaite, into the devil's infarction?
Are we animal, vegetable, mineral? Are
we paper, scissors, or stone? Are we a key
locked in someone else's box?

DORA

You ought to go feed the neighbor cats.
The contract says ninety-nine years.

    *Pause.*

That face at the bottom of the lake haunts
me, that face that so resembled your
father. Raymond had a way with practical
jokes, when he was younger. That was a
side of him you never saw. It's a pity
too. He lost whatever sense of humor he
possessed after the failure of the first
machine he invented, the Microscopic Midas
Tactoreceptor. Took the wind out of his
sails, so to speak. I always suspected
his faith was thinner than mine, and only

a thin coverlet hiding a despair. Such
things could not be parsed in church talk,
and I've always felt it best with sleeping
dogs to let be. Rabid ones you blast with
a shotgun from a safe distance.

    *She laughs.*

Raymond though, Raymond used to do the
most amusing things with department store
mannequins. You can't imagine! The human
body never dreamed of it, I'm sure. Once
he constructed a complete demonic diorama,
starring the Mayor, the City Council, and
 ladies from the Garden Club. Our goat,
Jasper, was featured prominently also.
It did not amuse many. Or the simulated,
hacked corpses he had a way of half-hiding
in more remote regions of Gooner Park. It
was a form of humor long on dark dare, and
provocation, and short on justifying higher
purpose. That's when the "devil" talk began.

    *We hear a music softly.*

SUSANNAH
    Does any of this MEAN anything, Mom?
    I mean, if all of us have an inescapable
    penchant for acts that defy convention,
    actions conceived in woe and bastardy,
    and consummated in direct contradiction
    to human nature? Aren't we standing in
    a perilous relation to our own destinies
    even, not to mention the high regard

of the community of Gradual, where we
reside?

DORA

Don't go and get metaphysical on me, Susannah.
Keep your mind fixed on the here and now,
things like feeding the cats, and so forth.
Which reminds me, I've got to look into the
matter of Raymond's insurance, to see if it
specifically declares null and void acts of
breakthrough into insubstantiation, even if
miraculously initiated. Me oh my.

SUSANNAH

I don't understand, Mother.

DORA

Neither do I, Susannah, and that's the sad
truth.

SUSANNAH

But I really want to, I really do.

DORA

Study grass. Study lace. Study the pattern
in these things. The truth is needlework. All
the rest is crotchety supposition. But the whole
world's at sixes and sevens, especially
what with this recent instance of Raymond's
translation into the faery world of the transmundane.
Faith is garbage, hog food, slops.

*She gets up suddenly, very agitated.*

SUSANNAH

Mother, how can you say that?* Mother, you
of all people?

DORA

Faith is a tale told by an idiot in a basement
during a bargain basement tale—I mean *sale.*

SUSANNAH

Belief is supposed to make you fine-boned,
and I'd feel anxious without any of it.

DORA

Believe me, the world goes whirling along
quite nicely without much of it, Susannnah.

SUSANNAH

But no it doesn't, don't you see?

DORA

All I want to know is why, why things
have got to be this way. Why I must live
in total disharmony with nature. Why I hate
this awful, spreading tub of dough that is
my human flesh. Why I wish to punish my
elders with pointless mockery, and tear
the bread from out of their mouths. What
I am doing on the face of this planet
when I cannot think of a moment in my life
that has not been shadowed by a failure
to follow through, to answer act with
any other strategy than timid, tactical
inaction, by the failure to connect.

SUSANNAH

I don't know what to say, mother.

DORA

Then for the love of Christ, shut up, Susannah.★
Just shut up.

*She sits down, terribly vexed.*

SUSANNAH

I thought America was supposed to be a happy
place. A place of bounty, and faith, and
problem-resolution through prudent self-interest.

DORA *(fiercely)*

Cut the crap, Susannah. Don't play innocent.
I see through your mask. Your pride and
selfish vaunting. The devil's working his
thick, hot, red tongue between your lips
even as we sit here. He makes you speak
such rot as would make me spew if I didn't
know well enough to not listen. Behind
those pale, thin lips. Those liquid, soft
does' eyes.★ Those perfect pearly teeth.

SUSANNAH

I'm not what you think, Mother. I'm not
thinking *that*. It's not true. Believe me.

DORA

Oh yes you are. I've known what you are
since I heaved you out of my belly, bloody,
bellowing, and full of shame.

SUSANNAH

Mother, I'm just an ordinary young
woman. I would never think those
things.

DORA

Yes, you would, you cheap slut. You
would because you are my daughter,
flesh of my flesh. So talk straight

123

and don't fool with me. You hear, Susannah?

SUSANNAH

All right, I *do* think those things. The
same things you think.★ Only I don't say them.

DORA

The very same things I think, Susannah?
You had better be sure they are exactly the
same, Susannah. Because if they are not
the very same things, then I promise you
I shall curse heart and soul till the
moon come down out of the sky, tear
your heart out while you yet live, and
you shall watch as she fry it in her skillet
and press the fat, red flesh in her mouth.

SUSANNAH

Mother, I promise never to say them.★ Again.

DORA

You promise, Susannah? Not ever?
Are you very sure?★ You must be very sure,
Susannah?

SUSANNAH

Cross my heart. Not ever.

    *Pause.*

SUSANNAH

Mother?

DORA

I've answered six of seven. That's enough
for tonight. There's work to be done. Let's
go.

*They rejoin the* MEN, *and the previous scene circles its square and completes itself. Pause. The* WOMEN *clear off the table while the* MAN *sits there, like an insensate thing. A boulder. Lights go down, then slowly come up on early morning of the next day. The music has of course, stopped and we hear the chirping of birds. Blackout.*


*Scene the next [* XX *(exxon)]: The* MAN, *seated as before is eating his breakfast.* SUSANNAH *pours some coffee for herself, and him. She has a few questions for him as well. Scene begins as he examines what's in his bowl carefully, extracts something large and dark from it with thumb and forefinger. He rapidly conveys this to his mouth, as if he were afraid it might be alive. He tucks a napkin into his collar, and chews doggedly on this object through the rest of the scene. His face is lowered, forward and tilted down, intent upon his work; his eyes are opened wide, rolled back and staring upward.* SUSANNAH *slowly dries a dish, a saucer perhaps, with a dishtowel. Thus occupied she walks slowly, downstage, to a far corner of the kitchen; in fact, as far from him as possible, probably along the rooms's diagonal. She crooks her head over her shoulder, and in this somewhat awkward position, addresses him. Outside* DORA'*s face is visible in the window.*

SUSANNAH

Do you intend to stay with us? Do you
intend to stay with us for some time?
How long?

*Fifteen-second pause.*

MR. WILLIAM HARD
Yes.

*Five-second pause.*

SUSANNAH
Answer my question. Exactly how long?

*Fifteen-second pause.*

MR. WILLIAM HARD
For ninety-nine years.

*He points to the suitcase.*

It says so in the contract.

*Fifteen second pause.*
*She points to the suitcase.*

SUSANNAH
What have you got in there?

*He snaps his fingers. The suitcase opens. A hoard of ordinary, but very rumpled clothing falls out. MOM rushes in, repacks the clothes, closes the suitcase, composes herself and goes out again. Her face reappears at the window.*

SUSANNAH
What do you want from us?

*Fifteen-second pause.*

What do you want, please tell me.

*Fifteen-second pause. Still no reply.*

Will you sleep with my mother?

*Her MOM's face disappears.*

Answer my question. Will you sleep★ with her?

MR. WILLIAM HARD
Yes.

*Fifteen-second pause.*

SUSANNAH
You really intend to sleep with her?

MR. WILLIAM HARD
Yes.

SUSANNAH
Will you fuck her?

*Thirty-second pause.*

MR. WILLIAM HARD
Yes.

*Thirty-second pause.*

SUSANNAH
Will you fuck me?

*Thirty-second pause.*

MR. WILLIAM HARD
Yes, if you want me to, and I
think I can get away with it.

*Thirty-second pause.*
*Both look down. The room is filled with shame.*

SUSANNAH
I don't want you to.

*Thirty-second pause.*

MR. WILLIAM HARD
Then I won't.

*Five-second pause.*
*Both visibly relax.*

SUSANNAH

Now that we've got that settled . . .

> *They hear music outdoors. It is* MAD WU. *The* MAN *arises,*
> *takes whatever it is he's been chewing on out of his mouth,*
> *places it carefully back in the bowl, and walks to the window.*
> *He looks out, then turns to* SUSANNAH. *She joins him at the*
> *window. A fifteen second pause as both look. He puts his hand*
> *on her shoulder. They look at each other, then out the window.*

SUSANNAH

Who is that man Mom is talking to?
Why is he making such a racket?

MR. WILLIAM HARD

That's Mad Wu, the Chinaman, from
the other end of the world.

SUSANNAH

Mad Wu, the Chinaman!

MR. WILLIAM HARD

Don't worry. He only calls himself that. He's
a harmless vagabond. From over in Corntown.
Where they buried the angel, or was it the devil?
in the calabashes . . .

> *Fifteen-second pause.*
> *She steps away, turns back and looks hard at him.*
> *Fifteen-second pause.*

SUSANNAH

Who are you, *really*? Tell me.

> *Fifteen-second fade to black, as* MAD WU's *music swells.*

*Scene the [ 𝄋𝄋𝄋 (willowy)]:* MAD WU *plays a song for*
DORA *who sits on a swing nearby, obviously enjoying herself.*
MAD WU *is dressed with great elegance. Evening clothes, and*
*wireless microphone. He sings his odd song with all the*
*assurance of a professional:*

MAD WU:

When the moon comes up
Motels are full of saxophones
of bingo bingo bam bango bum bim.

When the moon comes up
I think of my darling,
Hot, in the blue light.

Out there on Bug River
Motels full of pale travellers,
Lost within sight

Of bingo bingo bam bango bum bem.
Remind me of another time
When the moon came up.

In the motel of mind
I rehearse each night a scene
Of lover's horror:

Those who betrayed us
To love another run naked
With their red tongue bright.

And I grow lonesome
Without my wicked lover's
Head upon the pillow.

> I sleep in the woods
>    all day, all night.
> If I don't finish this song
>    There is no one around
> To tell me I'm wrong;
>    Or, worse, that I'm right.

And the hours I lost,
Spilled like spit on the salt earth
When the good take leave

Of the Bug River dead;
When the moon comes up and mourns
For bingo bingo bam bango bem bum.

but Bug River blazes bright.
And we who taste the hour
Of bingo bingo bam bango bem bum bim.

Curse the moonlight, curse
Like devils, on the white road
Of bingo bingo bam bango bum bim.

. . .

But when the moon sinks
We raise high the hopeless glass
Of black wine and drink.

When the moon comes up
On our explosive heartache
Set off the bomb.

SET OFF THE BOMB.

> I sleep in the woods
>     all day, all night;
> If I don't finish this song
>     There is no one around
> To tell me I'm wrong;
>     or, worse, that I'm right.

*As the song ends,* MOM *begins her monologue.* MAD WU
*continues his playing which provides an impromptu
accompaniment for her performance as well, different as it is
from his; all during this we behold a glorious sunset. While she
is soliloquizing, the* MAN *and the* DAUGHTER *steal out the
kitchen door, and into the vast, open spaces of the unexplored
back yard (this is the front yard).*

DORA

Say what you like, there is nothing like
music to fever the soul when the chill
of strangeness is upon it. It's like at
the crutch factory when they installed the
Distichous Musical Trip-hammer, or "D.M.T."

> *Pause.*

Say what you like, I should very much
like a very long vacation, a vacation
to someplace where no one has formed
the higher concept of "vacuum cleaner,"

or "dish washing" or "ironing board."
I think this place ought to be visually
hyposensitive, like certain of the cold,
dry valleys of Mars, or Antarctica, for
that matter; and be an ecological exacta
of hysteron-proteron. An edenic idyll
of hydrophane, where fruits abound, vice
is sweetly ignored, and our faithless
wonder in other people's fatuity bars
the hangman as surely as it beckons
to colorful birds like macaws and toucans,
lorries, parrots and lorikeets as they dodge
and sway, high above the vine-canopy, the
coral sea and our own wind-slathered fields
of automatic, self-harvesting wheat. I
feel a proper paradise ought to be perpetually
self-correcting, a reflexive, introspective
*perpetuum mobile* rather like Plato's
*Republic,* only with people like me,
roughly, on top. People with my tastes
roughly, on top. People with my tastes,
temper, sensitivity and degree of education.
Nothing more or less would be pleasant.

   *Pause for reflexion.*

As for the moon, I would have twelve
and be done with it. Each a different
size, shape, texture and color. They
would be arranged, artistically with orbits
of varying distance, ellipticality, period,
and grace. I would name them: Welk (after
Lawrence), Dorothy (after Oz), Isabella
(after the Queen of Castille), Amelia (after

the obvious), Turkey, Tonsil, Okra, Banana,
Lace, Greedy, Moth, Pretzel, Dog and Dudu.
That's two too many, but then again two
of the twelve could be double-named; or
possess a secret life while coasting around
the other end of creation.

     *Pause for a bad thought.*

Oh my. Identity is a hellish burden. I'm
completely fed up with the whole thing.
Parenting, wifing, the PTA, the Democratic
Party (liberalism), then the Republican
Party (conservatism), then the party of
Ross Perot (geezer politics), highways,
house paint, salad bowls, exercise machines,
aerobics, lack of exercise, the Garden Club,
licence plates, television, night-vision,
VCRs, Robot cheese, coathangers, paperclips,
other people, mystery novels, romance novels,
novels period, other people, anything that
is packaged in a way safe for children,
garbage bags full of stuff, empty garbage
bags, garbage, bags, sunglasses, reading
glasses, glasses, glass, other people,
not being able to see, toothpaste, oil
for the skin, oil for salad, cooking oil,
gasoline, oil companies, hospitals, smells
that remind one of hospital smells, illness,
pain, the suffering of others, the pleasure
of others, other people. The trap of being
something definite. A woman in middle of
her life surrounded by people who feel
nothing. Who feel literally nothing! A

slight curvature of the spine. A desperation
for pocket money. A loathing for other people's
ash-trays, toenail clippings, and tendency to
burp. God contains bad stuff. One swell
foop. An embarrassment of clichés.

*She looks down at herself, and softly wails.*

What bloody-minded god dreamt up
this female mishap of bad-plumbing?
Cysts, fibroids, yeast infections. Swellings
and drainings. Tumescence, cramps and
detumescences. A horror-show cycle of
fecundity, and the wobble of fertility.
The unsteadiness of having to endure
what one has not willed for oneself. Children!
Children who turn into strangers. The
once welcoming world that turns its back
once you come into your gray maturity,
once you understand your need. Baffling,
it midasizes every hope, each slender dream
into the solid elemental dross of regret.
Midas backwards transposed. So much,
everything! all that I've chosen. Even
when I chose truly, I chose wrong. The
young and female are right to put off
all choosing. Yet not to choose is
worse. Because then the choosing is done
for you, societally, institutionally,
by your family, husband, colleagues,
social betters, or those persons far
away, who design the argument of your
future needs, even before you are
aware. People far away, who never

rest, who know your heart, mind and
every little itch better than you
ever will and have the courtesy not
to tell you what they know till you've
taken the trouble to put your cash
down, plunk, on the table. True power
dropped to the subterranean layer of
taste, fashion, what clothes, what hair
color and length, this book or that
(both truly awful), this drug or that
(both with truly terrifying side-effects),
 lotto number. Vibrator speed. What
docudrama or infomercial that touched
us too deeply when we were tipsy, that
plucked the fatal heartstring, once,
when your guard was down, and you went
unwary into the pandemonium of the world,
its hospitals, its supermarkets, its
country clubs. Its malls with their
vile urchins, filth and muffled din.

> *She holds her ears. He has stopped playing and is looking at her, intently. She realizes she has been going on a little.*

DORA

This is silly. I shouldn't talk too much.

MAD WU

It sounds crazy, coming from someone like you.

DORA

I'm sorry. I should watch my behavior.

MAD WU

Your behavior can take care of itself. Leave
it alone.

DORA

I don't have anything today for you.

MAD WU

I'm not *you*. I'm Wu. And since I come
from China, I don't need anything. In
China the trees grow upside-down.

DORA

Here's a dollar. Go away. You're disturbing me.

MAD WU

Look, I am a folksy and amusing antitype
to the contemporary cliché of the homeless
person as a pathetic, scrofulous, deranged
drug-ravaged glossalalian *sauvage* and ultimate
social victim. I'm invoking the previous
cliché of the wise, mad fool, and it works.
The poison of the latter neutralizes the poison
of the former. My true character is conditional.

> *He bows.*

Conditional, contingent, conventional, and
phantasmal. I am here for the purpose of
singing a song. Which I have successfully
accomplished. My mission now, that being
done, is, like yours, one of escape.

> *He produces a map.*

I suggest we rusticate ourselves to the town
of Moon Hat, some seventeen miles down Route
6, as the crow flies, also adjacent Bug River
but further North, direction of the devil,
but closer to its source among the Ice Mountains.

I suppose you've never heard of Moon Hat.

MAD WU

DORA

I'll take your word for it.

MAD WU

I wouldn't if I were you. I'm a congenital liar.

DORA

If you hate America enough to make such a
spectacle of yourself that's good enough
for me.

MAD WU

One thing, I don't believe in flashbacks,
freezeframes, or time-lapse cinematography.

DORA

Fine with me.

MAD WU

Everything is fine with you. How do you
expect to get through life if you're not
more complex? The world is complex. It
contains things like "tantalum" and the
large intestine; it contains things like
the Omaha Subharmonic Lantern Wheel. Also
known as O.S.L . . .

DORA

That's an invention of Raymond's. A dream
of his anyway. Before he went subcritical.
The Omaha Subharmonic Lantern★ Wheel is . . .

*She looks at him hard. He looks at her hard.*

MAD WU

Don't get all moony on me now. I'm serious.

137

DORA

Wait just a minute. I want to take off my apron.

*He grabs her hand.*

MAD WU

Keep it, there are dirty dishes in Moon Hat too.

DORA

I don't know if I should do this.

*He begins to play his music. She looks up at the moon.*

MAD WU

The Moon Hattans are not from Manhattan.
They are realists. They have certain down-home
needs too.

DORA

I hunger so much for what I
will never be able to understand.

MAD WU

Join the crowd.

DORA

What will everyone think of me
 if I just up and leave, without
so much as a note, a hint, or
the most perfunctory fare-the-well?

MAD WU

They'll pack up all their belongings
in wheelbarrows. They'll follow you.
Escape is useless, but escape from escape
is even worse. My, look at that moon.

DORA

So, you're teasing me?

MAD WU

Pardon me, I am from China, all
the way around the world. Your physics
means nothing to me. But I do know
I am an unnatural entity, and that
when I cease to have anything to say
the only recourse is to vacate the
premises. This distinguishes me from
all Americans. But then the theatre
of Gradual possesses other charms . . .

*Pause.*

Dead dogs, for instance. Cats and rabid raccoons.

*She throws down her apron.*

DORA

Okay, okay. I'm coming.

MAD WU

I'm going to lead you to the stars, Dora.
I'm going to take you where you've
never been, to the blackberry bog at
East Moon Hat. Where people still
wear the kilts and fezzes native to
the region, where they still employ
the Univocal Sine-Wave Perforator
to crack open hickory nuts, where folks
gather in secret to worship St Lachesis,
patron saint of legalized gambling.★
Where we shall toast to Peace, Harmony,
and Selective Immortality, at the classy

lounges and establishments of Moon Hat.
[It isn't] We shall sip silvery martinis
by an art deco mirror that reflects our
nullity and reverses our sappy question-mark
into a universal affirmation suitable for
framing, family-viewing and . . . so forth.

DORA

That doesn't sound like America.

    *Pause.*

I have the feeling this has all happened
before. Long ago and far away.★ I'm . . .
so happy . . .

MAD WU

It most certainly did. History occurs first
as tragedy, then is repeated successively
as farce, crime, and flim-flam. Then,
when all hope is gone, as . . . forgetfulness.

    *It's dark now. They begin to go out.*

DORA

That's just what I mean . . . my word,
would you get a load of that moon? No,
I mean it's so *exhilarating*★ not to know . . .

MAD WU

You got it, baby. The well of stupidity is
bottomless. Ignorance, true ignorance
shames the infinite with its extent, its
sheer maximal scope. Embrace your
ignorance. It'll never let you★ down.

DORA

Look, look at the moon!

MAD WU

Why, what for?

DORA

It looks so real it almost looks fake.

MAD WU

You can say that again.

DORA

. . . looks so real it almost looks fake . . .

MAD WU

I've heard that before.

DORA

What's that supposed to mean?

MAD WU

. . . could be . . .

DORA

. . . jerk . . .

> *Go out arm in arm.*
> *Blackout is complete.*


> *Lights up in the backyard. Scene:* [〰〰(tigertiger)]. *The man is lugging his suitcase talking all the while to Susannah who is guiding him carefully with a flashlight.*

MR. WILLIAM HARD

. . . and the corn of Asaph was buried
in the ditch with Japeth and Gamaliel;

and they are come into the Land of Evening
and lay down upon the ground; and Garth
and Starfish went to Zenith with Altazimuth
and begat the tribe of Starfish;
and these too are come into the
Land of Evening where they all
lay down upon the ground; and
Fishhead Curry talked with Tobit
concerning the doings of Ashtaroth,
and it grew even to the Seventh
Hour of the day, then She came—
She, in her gown of nitre and wormwood—
and they were pacified; and threw
down their idols of wood and tantalum,
and drove their flocks into the Land
of Evening whereupon they all took
off their shoes, and lay down upon
the hard ground; and the High Lords
of Ckm Ckm, both blood-eating and
truly Dradical, met the Dark One,
Azazzael who pitched the cup of hot
custard in their faces, and made them
fall down and worship him, but Moab
met with Zechariah and Nebuchadnezzar
with Shenango, and all took an oath
under the shade of Whelk and Wheelbug,
and they knew the worm from what the
worm eats, and by this knowing they
cast lots, and Ishmael spoke to
Susannah and Suwannee in pidgin of
pignuts in pigpens, of pygmies in
saris kneeling before Sasquatch in
the sassafras, and knew by Worm-Hole

the wonders of worm-fence and caused
a worm-gear to be builded upon the
sand of Isfahan and Durango; these,
too, they all dropped their tools
in the ditch and walked with slow, mystic
tread into the Land of Evening and there
they rested their hot pads, and they
all lay down on the Earth, yea, all
lay down amongst the nettles and
prickly pear, before the Tabernacle
of the Mighty One, the one whose name
is X forever and a day, till all the
pig iron in Mimbreland is changed to
*penicillium;* and . . . so forth . . .

SUSANNAH

Bill? Why do you need a shovel? Are you
going to dig up something? This is where
I buried my goldfish when I was a kid.
This is where I buried the angelfish.
And this . . .

>    *Another spot.*

. . . is where Dad buried Richard M. Nixon
when he was excommunicated by the House of
Reprehensibles, in New Pork City . . .
New York City, I mean. That was back
in '77. Dad didn't actually bury the
President, it was only an effigy, a
Richard M. Nixon doll. We walked around
the house: Mom, Dad, Simon, and me. In
the dark. Like now. Beating on roasting
pans and buckets with soup spoons and

rolling pins. Dad mutilated the effigy
in horrible ways while I smeared ketchup
all over it. Then by torchlight (we
had made improvised torches out of brooms,
tar and kerosene) we buried it here,
howling. We trampled on the grave with
our pants down. Dad told us not to tell
anyone at school. Especially at the
Guidance Office. So I didn't. It was
really neat. And yuky—neat and yuky—
at the same time. It goosewillied me
severely.

*His wild eyes are bright.*

MR. WILLIAM HARD
This must be where they buried the Angel.

SUSANNAH
Angelfish. I told you.

MR. WILLIAM HARD
No, no, no. It's from an old prophecy.
From the Book of Folding Chairs. The
High Molality of Sacro Lumbar. An angel
fell here, the book says: " . . . twenty
snake-skins from the Bug River by the
town of Whangdoodle . . ." —and that's
Gradual, in the parlance of the Torrid
Zealots. So it's got to be here . . .
but where?

*He looks about.*

Saint Modred the Tormentor. A very wicked
saint from Shenango who began his days in

the dry goods business, and was known in
the period before his conversion as the
inventor of the Semi-Square Nickel-Plate
May-Wine Pile-Driver, used to send telegraph
messages to those hypothetical beings we
call "the niggle-carp people," at the
center of the world. In the boiling atomic
madness of the core. Right through the
Mohorovicic Discontinuity and everything,
and that takes some technological knowhow,
I assure you. Then he went mad.★ Then he . . .

SUSANNAH
That was no angel, that was my brother,
Simon.

*But he's not listening.*

MR. WILLIAM HARD
He also invented the Pygmy Klein Bottle.
But Mister Klein had the better attorneys,
and patented it first.

SUSANNAH
I told you—that's where we scattered Simon's
ashes.

MR. WILLIAM HARD
Your brother was Saint Modred the Tormentor?

SUSANNAH
No, he was Simon Moredent, of our family,
of the family of Moredent. He was dealing
drugs at Gradual High. He was a genius,
but his talents went to waste. He died
one night in June. His girl friend broke

off with him because he was destroying his
mind with drugs.

MR. WILLIAM HARD
Drugs are a terrible thing.

SUSANNAH
He was so desperate he stole a semi from
the A&P. On top of that he took an
overdose of crack cocaine. On top of
that the truck jack-knifed up on Route
6, in the rain. On top of that he was
struck by lightning as he lay there,
dying, all broken and bloody, all zonked
out on drugs. It was terrible. He was
a genius. When he wasn't on drugs he
was the most beautiful person in the
world. He wrote a little poem for me:
"When the moon comes up
        . . ."

> *He looks very wild. He cuts her off.*

MR. WILLIAM HARD
Never mind. Never mind. Poetry is for
idiots. This brother of yours might
have been the one. And if he *is*, this
is the spot.

> *He dumps his stuff, and begins to dig. Stops. Goes through his*
> *pockets till he finds some papers. Grabs the flashlight from her*
> *and studies them. He produces calipers and measures something*
> *on one of the papers, a scribbled map.*

SUSANNAH
Who are you really, Bill?

*He ignores her.*

You haven't come here because
of my brother.

*An unholy pause.*

MR. WILLIAM HARD
Strange, there is corn all about the
place. Wild corn. I wonder why . . .

*Her notices her. Pause.*

SUSANNAH
Tell me what you have come here for.

*He kneels, looks down for fifteen seconds.*

Tell me, Bill.

MR. WILLIAM HARD
Do you know the story of the Fork and Spoon
who ran away?

SUSANNAH
No . . .

MR. WILLIAM HARD
Do you know the story of the man who became
a Cardinal to meet women?

SUSANNAH
No . . .

MR. WILLIAM HARD
Do you know the tale of the monster baby-sitting
scene? Or of the Hyacinth Macaw, the Sulphur-Crested
Cockatoo, and the Concave-Casqued Hornbill? Or
of what *really* transpired at the Evil Santas' workshop?

SUSANNAH
No. No. No.

MR. WILLIAM HARD
Then why should I trust anything you say?
Or put any faith in your judgment?

SUSANNAH
—

MR. WILLIAM HARD
—

> *She looks down, clenches her fists and lets out with a terrible cry, half sob, half whoop. He reaches out to hold her.*

SUSANNAH
Don't touch my butt in public.

MR. WILLIAM HARD
Sorry. All Presocratics have furry hands.

> *She turns and hisses, stopping only when she notices the moon, tremendous, pale and weird. He stands tall.*

What do I care about your damnable brother?

SUSANNAH
Well I did, and do.

MR. WILLIAM HARD
Life goes on, Susannah. Get over it.

> *She sighs*

SUSANNAH
Want to hear my theory?★ I think all things . . .

MR. WILLIAM HARD

Susannah, look at the moon and what
do you see? Look! Look hard . . .

SUSANNAH

I see the moon. Big deal. What's so special
about that?* Can we just move on . . .

MR. WILLIAM HARD

No, Susannah, that is *not* what we see.
That is what we think we see, but, alas
the optic on the lunar is not a true
apparence.

    *Pause.*

It's flim-flam.

SUSANNAH

What are you suggesting, Bill?

    *Fifteen-second pause.*
    *Slowly, he points at the moon.*

MR. WILLIAM HARD

It's all a hoax.

SUSANNAH

A hoax?

MR. WILLIAM HARD

A swindle, yes.

SUSANNAH

A swindle?

MR. WILLIAM HARD

Yes, I would say. A deception.

*Pause. She laughs.*

The optic on the lunar possesses
an aspect of moonliness, but not
its essence. It's a fake. I'll show you.

> *She doubles up with laughter as he scrambles up stage. By dint
> of much clambering he nears the moon. He taps on it with his
> fingernail. We hear auditory proof that* BILL *is correct: this
> moon is a fake. She is stunned.* SUSANNAH *holds her cheeks in
> her hands.*

SUSANNAH
Wow.

> *He climbs down, straightens out his clothing, and comes
> downstage to her. He hands her a letter. Pause. She opens and
> reads it.*

MR. WILLIAM HARD
It's a fake. A duplicate. A mere replica.

> *She looks at him hard.*

SUSANNAH
What happened to the moon? The real moon,
I mean.

MR. WILLIAM HARD
The real moon is dying.

> *Thirty-second pause.*

SUSANNAH
Oh.

> *He leans close to her.*

MR. WILLIAM HARD

The moon is in my suitcase. And you
might as well hear it all, now that
you have learned a part.

*He stands tall.*

I've come from the Land of Evening, here,
with the moon in my suitcase. The moon
has nearly expired, and I am—with
your assistance—going to bury the moon
on the spot. According to an ancient
rule . . .

*She looks back at the letter. She reads. Pause.*

SUSANNAH

What's a "tarboosh"?

*He hands her one. She takes it. He puts on his own. Pause.
She puts on hers.*

Tell me more. This is fascinating.

*He begins to dig the grave. She holds the flashlight for him.*

MR. WILLIAM HARD

In the time of Zed and Zeph people were
stupid and slow, but because of gradualness
they were graceful. And goodheartedness★
was not a mere . . . fillip.

SUSANNAH

Wait a minute. You opened your suitcase
for me. Before. I saw what was inside. I'm
not so stupid. What was inside was clothes.

MR. WILLIAM HARD
False-bottom.

*She looks at him hard.*

SUSANNAH
Show me.

*He looks down, thinking. He looks up.*

MR. WILLIAM HARD
When the time comes.

SUSANNAH
Show me now.

*Fifteen-second pause.*

MR. WILLIAM HARD
All right.

*He opens, very slowly, the suitcase, only a sliver. A terrible light bathes them both for thirty seconds. We hear the ancient melody of YU KO. He closes the suitcase. Both stand.*

SUSANNAH
Wow.

MR. WILLIAM HARD
Ultimately, Susannah, to doubt is to do
a very bad thing with your head.

SUSANNAH
Maybe we're all duplicates.

*He takes up the shovel and starts to work.*

MR. WILLIAM HARD
The philosopher Plato thought so.

*He digs for some time.*

SUSANNAH

> . . . my theory is that all people give off
> a glow. A strange, barely perceptible
> glow. This glow is the furnace of life.
> Over the ages the glow will slowly
> become brighter and brighter, and more
> apparent. Then one day each one of us
> will slip out of our mortal human body,
> and drop it to the ground, like an old
> sock or glove. Like a garment we no
> longer need. The world will be called
> "Ding-Dong" and people will glide high
> above the surface of the earth, like the
> angels once did, walking light on the
> spongy pathways of aire!

MR. WILLIAM HARD

> Hallelujah!

SUSANNAH

> Like box-kites with a brain. Or like
> big, ectoplasmic bats. Fabulous bats.

> *He goes back to work. Pause.*

> In some people the glow is more pronounced
> than others. In some the glow is very dim.

MR. WILLIAM HARD

> Devil raise a hump upon this hard earth.

SUSANNAH

> I can see the glow on my skin, sometimes,
> on my belly. On my cheeks and arms.

MR. WILLIAM HARD
The glow is also a gradual process.

SUSANNAH
People who are dim are disgusting. They
crouch low and huddle in the square boxes
of their shabby lives. I think people
who have no glow ought to be exterminated.
Shot in the streets and be left to molder
there, or be cast down with John Moldy,
in his basement.

MR. WILLIAM HARD
—

SUSANNAH
—

*Pause. Sky becomes bright for a moment. Then it darkens
again. Pause.*

. . . WOW . . .

MR. WILLIAM HARD
The Great Vegetarian thought so too.

SUSANNAH
Who was the Great Vegetarian?

MR. WILLIAM HARD
Adolf Hitler.

SUSANNAH
But he was a very bad man.

MR. WILLIAM HARD
Yes, he was, Susannah.

*He digs very hard.*

SUSANNAH

They are to be shot. Strangled. Stabbed
with the long, silvery spindle of a dagger.
In the heart.

MR. WILLIAM HARD

Only what is slow can absorb all
the poison we emit. Poisons of the
head. Poisons of the heart. In a
million years none of this will
matter.

SUSANNAH

I don't care about what the world
will be like then. Do you need some
help?

MR. WILLIAM HARD

I need you to hold that flashlight.

SUSANNAH

What's that thing down there?

MR. WILLIAM HARD

Hard . . . damn . . .

SUSANNAH

What's that thing there?

MR. WILLIAM HARD

The shadow. Of my foot. Nothing.

SUSANNAH

How deep does the grave have to be?

MR. WILLIAM HARD

Not too deep fortunately.

SUSANNAH

Guess the moon doesn't need a coffin.

MR. WILLIAM HARD

The moon has no arms and legs.

*She whistles while he digs. We hear the wind in the trees. She turns to him.*

SUSANNAH

You never explained why you had to
bury the moon.

MR. WILLIAM HARD

Why did you have to bury your
brother Simon?

SUSANNAH

Leave Simon out of it, okay? Besides,
we didn't bury Simon, we scattered his
ashes . . .

MR. WILLIAM HARD

I am a Diophantine Intrilligator, I don't
have to explain anything.

*Pause.*

SUSANNAH

So . . . what do you think of my theory?

MR. WILLIAM HARD

We are all sleepwalkers in a boiling
furnace of flame.

SUSANNAH

What do you do for fun? Listen to music,
go dancing? Do you play cards?

*Shivers.*

It's getting chilly. Will you be done soon?

MR. WILLIAM HARD
Okay, we're ready. I need your help.

SUSANNAH
What do I do?

*He opens the suitcase. Light!*

MR. WILLIAM HARD
It's very heavy. And I've brought a towel.
Hold it through the towel. Otherwise
you'll burn your hands. Even in its
current state the moon is very hot.

*She touches it gingerly.*

SUSANNAH
Wow, it sure is.

MR. WILLIAM HARD
Ready?

SUSANNAH
Well, okay.

*Together they lift the moon, wrapped in a bath towel. It is
about the size of a basketball. Even wrapped the moon glows
with odd intensity.*

God, it's heavy.

MR. WILLIAM HARD
It is heavy. Lead, nickel and antimony mainly.
And tantalum . . .

*Slowly they lower the moon into the grave. It takes some doing owing to the spherical shape of the moon, and the need to keep it covered.*

Easy, easy . . .

SUSANNAH
  . . . have you got it?

MR. WILLIAM HARD
  Okay, you can let go.

SUSANNAH
  . . . goosewillies me . . .

    *Pause. He secures the moon where he wants it to rest.*

MR. WILLIAM HARD
  Good. We're almost done.

    *Both stand up and straighten out their arms and legs. They stretch.*

SUSANNAH
  Do you . . . have you ever done things like this . . . before?

    *He looks at her.*

MR. WILLIAM HARD
  :—

SUSANNAH
  :—

MR. WILLIAM HARD
  Now just a little shovelling and we'll be done.

    *She turns to face out, as the* MAN *shovels dirt in the grave. Slowly she raises her arms, and pronounces a mock benediction in a quiet voice.*

SUSANNAH:

Let the Parsley rejoice with Dinoflagellate;
  For the dip-needle knows nothing of the Crow.
Let the Sultanate of Swish be florous with Alphabets;
  For Amoebic Dysentery is awash with Amatol.
Let Comparison Shop walk with Depressor Nerve;
  For Paragoge is wink and wingnut with Kemal Ataturk.
Let Borax be titanous with tidbit and tizzy;
  For all the names of Shenango are gradual.
Let Forenoon worship with Calamity Jane;
  For the Quizmaster quits in the name of Sheboygan.
Let Spun Glass and Sprocket speak with Leland Stanford;
  For Grandma Moody officiates in panic and panfry.
Let Pangloss worship with the Erie Canal;
  For Panic Button panhandles the Photogravure.

> *He's done now as the blackout begins. Both look down at the grave with respect. They both cross themselves. He lays the shovel on the grave. She holds her hand over her heart.*

MR. WILLIAM HARD

Now we all, each and every one, are orphans.

> *Pause.*

SUSANNAH

May Misrule and Hepcat be conjugate . . . . with . . .
The Hyacinth Macaw. Ipso Facto. La. La la.

> *Black out.*

END OF PLAY

# MAC WELLMAN

Described by the *New York Times* as "a playwright intoxicated with words," Mac Wellman has written over thirty plays, two novels, and several collections of poetry. Among his recent plays are *7 Blowjobs* (performed at Soho Rep in New York and at San Diego's Sledgehammer Theatre); *Sincerity Forever* (commissioned by the Roger Nathan Hirsch Award for the Unicorn Theatre at the Berkshire Theatre Festival; and subsequently produced by BACA Downtown, New York, and at the Frank Theatre in Minneapolis); *Three Americanisms* (performed at the Soho Rep); *Crowbar* (performed at the Victory Theatre on 42nd Street in New York); *Bad Penny* (performed in Manhattan's Central Park as part of En Garde's Central Park Service); *Albanian Softshoe* (at the San Diego Rep); and *Terminal Hip* (a solo piece for actor Steven Mellor, performed at P.S. 122 in New York). Wellman won a *Village Voice* Obie Award for *Bad Penny, Terminal Hip,* and *Crowbar* in 1990, and won another Obie for *Sincerity Forever* in 1991.

Among his many drama publications are the recent collection of plays, *The Bad Infinity: Eight Plays,* published by Johns Hopkins University Press; *Bad Penny* and *The Professional Frenchman,* both published by Sun & Moon Press; and *Harm's Way,* published by Broadway Play Publishing. He has also edited several collections of plays, including *Theater of Wonders* (Sun & Moon Press) and *7 Different Plays* (Broadway Play Publishing).

Wellman has also published several collections of poetry, *In Praise of Secrecy* (1977), *Satires* (1985), and *A Shelf in Woop's Clothing* (1990), among them. His novel, *The Fortuneteller,* was published by Sun & Moon in 1991.

He has received numerous grants, including awards from the McKnight and Rockefeller Foundations, and fellowships from the National Endowment for the Arts and the Guggenheim Foundation. He lives in Brooklyn with his wife, Yolanda Gerritson, a Dutch journalist.

## SUN & MOON CLASSICS

This publication was made possible, in part, through an operational grant from the Andrew W. Mellon Foundation and through contributions from the following individuals:

Charles Altieri (Seattle, Washington)
John Arden (Galway, Ireland)
Jesse Huntley Ausubel (New York, New York)
Dennis Barone (West Hartford, Connecticut)
Jonathan Baumbach (Brooklyn, New York)
Guy Bennett (Los Angeles, California)
Bill Berkson (Bolinas, California)
Steve Benson (Berkeley, California)
Charles Bernstein and Susan Bee (New York, New York)
Dorothy Bilik (Silver Spring, Maryland)
Bill Corbett (Boston, Massachusetts)
Fielding Dawson (New York, New York)
Robert Crosson (Los Angeles, California)
Tina Darragh and P. Inman (Greenbelt, Maryland)
David Detrich (Los Angeles, California)
Christopher Dewdney (Toronto, Canada)
Philip Dunne (Malibu, California)
George Economou (Norman, Oklahoma)
Elaine Equi and Jerome Sala (New York, New York)
Lawrence Ferlinghetti (San Francisco, California)
Richard Foreman (New York, New York)
Howard N. Fox (Los Angeles, California)
Jerry Fox (Aventura, Florida)
In Memoriam: Rose Fox
Melvyn Freilicher (San Diego, California)
Miro Gavran (Zagreb, Croatia)
Peter Glassgold (Brooklyn, New York)
Barbara Guest (New York, New York)
Perla and Amiram V. Karney (Bel Air, California)
Fred Haines (Los Angeles, California)
Fanny Howe (La Jolla, California)
Harold Jaffe (San Diego, California)
Ira S. Jaffe (Albuquerque, New Mexico)
Alex Katz (New York, New York)
Tom LaFarge (New York, New York)
Mary Jane Lafferty (Los Angeles, California)

If you would like to be a contributor to this series, please send your tax-deductible contribution to The Contemporary Arts Educational Project, Inc., a nonprofit corporation, 6026 Wilshire Boulevard, Los Angeles, California 90036.

RECENT BOOKS IN THE SUN & MOON CLASSICS

★First American publication
★★Revised edition

# AMERICAN THEATER IN LITERATURE (ATL)

Developed by The Contemporary Arts Educational Project, Inc., a nonprofit corporation, and published through its Sun & Moon Press, the American Theater in Literature program was established to promote American theater as a literary form and to educate readers about contemporary and modern theater. The program publishes work of major American playwrights as well as younger, developing dramatists in various publishing programs of the Press, including the Sun & Moon Classics (collections of plays of international significance), the Mark Taper Forum Plays, Soho Rep Plays, Undermain Theatre Plays, Primary Stages plays, and as a regular imprint of Sun & Moon Press.

BOOKS IN THIS PROGRAM

Len Jenkins *Dark Ride and Other Plays* ($13.95)
(Sun & Moon Classics: 22)
Robert Auletta *The Persians* ($9.95)
(A Mark Taper Forum Play)
Matthew Maguire *The Tower* ($8.95)
Kier Peters *The Confirmation* ($6.95)
Len Jenkin *Careless Love* ($9.95)
(A Soho Rep Play / Sun & Moon Classics: 54)
Mac Wellman *Two Plays: A Murder of Crows* and
*The Hyacinth Macaw* ($11.95)
(A Primary Stages Play / Sun & Moon Classics: 62)
Jeffrey Jones *Love Trouble* ($10.95)
(An Undermain Theatre Play / Sun & Moon Classics: 84)